MARKETING YOUR ARTS AND CRAFTS

Creative Ways
to *Profit* from Your Work

JANICE WEST

THE SUMMIT GROUP • FORT WORTH, TEXAS

THE SUMMIT GROUP

1227 West Magnolia, Suite 500, Fort Worth, Texas 76104

97 96 95 94   5 4 3 2 1

This publication is designed to provide accurate and authoritative information in regard to the subject matter covered. It is sold with the understanding that the publisher is not engaged in rendering legal, accounting, or other professional service. If legal advice or other expert assistance is required, the services of a competent professional person should be sought.

Library of Congress Cataloging-in-Publication Data
West, Janice.
    Marketing your arts and crafts: creative ways to profit from your work/Janice West.
    p.cm.
    ISBN 1-56530-127-7: $24.95
    1. Decorative arts—United States—Marketing. 2. Handicraft—United States—Marketing. I. Title.
NK805.W45 1994
745.5'068'8—dc20   94-5493
                                                                           CIP

Cover Credits:
Ceramic vase courtesy of LaDean, Fort Worth, Texas
Needlepoint by The Needlepoint Gallery, Fort Worth, Texas
Woodcarving by Robert Beverly, Arlington, Texas

To my parents, Mary and Jimmie Jirasek,
who have always been supportive of my efforts;
to my husband, Richard, who never doubted for one day, one hour, or
one minute that my notes would become a book,
and to my son, Derek, who makes all this worthwhile.

Table of Contents

User's Guide
Cross Reference

Acknowledgments

To Managing Editor Mike Towle, who always believed in my project, and to all the other members of The Summit Group for their energetic efforts in publishing and bringing this book to the marketplace.

My appreciation to Joyce, Alan, and Jonathan Kappeler for their encouragement, support, and wonderful Virginia hospitality. Very special regards to Dr. Cap Oliver and Charlene Henderson. Many thanks to Debbie Kessler, Mark Levine, and Dr. Alan Wasserman. Thanks to all the artists, craftsworkers, buyers, and other business professionals who so generously contributed their knowledge and expertise.

Introduction

If you are like most artists and craftspeople, you labor long hours perfecting your work. Then you have to turn around and spend even more hours trying to sell your creations. You probably became an artist or craftsperson because you love to create. However, you might not love the activities associated with selling. What this book does is provide the marketing knowledge that you as an artisan need to assist you in your business endeavors.

Marketing Your Arts and Crafts helps you locate numerous places that really want to buy arts and crafts. This book not only lists specific promising markets, but also shows the reader that it is not always essential to spend a lot of money in order to sell products successfully.

This book is designed to make the marketing process user-friendly. Fifty specific markets for arts and crafts are identified. As you read through this book you will find that there are many places searching for all types of work ranging from fine art to country crafts. While some buyers specify that they want to buy only certain items, others open their doors to all arts and crafts. Some of the ways listed in this book are for those who are just starting to sell their products. Other ways are for businesses that have been around long enough to be actively looking for growth opportunities.

Some common questions asked are:

■ *How do you find markets for your work?*
Buyers really want to acquire quality arts and crafts. In fact, quite often they cannot procure enough items to meet their customers' increasing demands. Businesses must constantly discover new products if they wish to survive. All over the world, buyers (from corporate curators to museum purchasing managers) actively search for quality arts and crafts work. So, when marketing your products, remember that boutiques, gift shops, and catalogs need your work just as much as you need access to their customers.

■ *How many markets for your work do you need?*
Often, success is possible by finding simply one mar-

ket that wants to buy all of your work. Kathy Wood, who buys for the seven gift shops of the Loews Anatole Hotel, tends to buy all of the work that the artisans she works with can produce. Sometimes, craftspeople sell all their work by one method only, such as through conventions or conferences. Edie Craig and Lynda Ault make "educational" aprons that they sell through state teachers' conventions. Right now that method of marketing brings them as much business as they want.

Others find that marketing their work in two or more ways is best for them. Jewelry artisan Lynne Rutherford sells her work at the Music Educators' Conference every February. She also holds "private jewelry showings" during holiday seasons as well. The number of markets that you choose to sell through ultimately depends on the nature of your product, your personal approach to selling, and your business goals.

■ *How do you determine which markets best suit your personal style of selling?*
Some artisans enjoy meeting customers face-to-face so they can better discover buyers' needs and desires. For those with outgoing personalities, demonstrating and selling products at the Handmade in America shows fits their needs perfectly. Others, who prefer to create in solitude, might want to fill orders that someone else—such as Americraft Gift Brokers—obtains from buyers. These artisans may also elect to hire a sales representative selected through the Rep Registry to sell their work. This book lists marketing ways designed to suit everyone's personal style of selling.

Marketing Your Arts and Crafts describes how to locate and gain access to all kinds of businesses seeking all kinds of products. Interviews with industry professionals are included so that you will have a better idea of their expectations. In addition, marketing-related topics of interest to artisans are addressed in special sections.

A wide range of marketing options for all types of artists and crafters, at every stage of business development, are provided in *Marketing Your Arts and Crafts*. As a craftsworker or artist you owe it to yourself and to those who will enjoy your creations to explore the enormous sales potential that exists. Such knowledge can enable you to take advantage of the abundant opportunities offered by these dynamic markets.

By the time you read this book, some of the information such as names, addresses, telephone numbers, dollar amounts, and other such material might have changed or be out of date. Please feel free to write me about any updating that might be necessary. I would also be interested in hearing about your personal selling experiences. I wish you success in all your endeavors. All correspondence should be addressed to: Janice West, P.O. Box 156555, Fort Worth, Texas 76155.

CHAPTER 1

Holiday House Boutiques

*Showcase your
Arts and Crafts
at
Holiday House
Boutiques*

PRODUCTS BUYERS WANT: arts and crafts

COSTS TO CONSIDER: Entry fees range from $10 to $150 per show. Show organizers also receive a fixed percentage of the selling price.

Holiday House Boutiques or Seasonal Boutiques are special craft shows ordinarily offered twice a year—Christmas and Spring (usually around Easter)—by different groups of people nationwide. Holiday House Boutiques sell large amounts of various merchandise ranging from seasonal decorations to functional artwork. As a rule, they are held in special locations, such as historical houses or even castles. These boutiques can also be organized and operated from individuals' homes or at school gymnasiums. Artists and crafters do not have to be present to sell their work. Items are taken or mailed to the Holiday House about two weeks before the show starts.

An organizer or promoter sells items on consignment in a Holiday House Boutique. Payment is received only when an item has been sold. In the case of Holiday House Boutiques, items are inventoried at the end of the affair and one check is usually issued for the total number of pieces sold. Unsold pieces are returned. Holiday House Boutique organizers are selective with the items they choose to show, so entrants must compete for acceptance.

SPECIAL FEATURE: Customers often wait in long lines for doors to open. These boutiques attract anywhere from several hundred to thousands of customers, depending on how long they have been in operation.

HOW TO CONTACT:	For a listing of boutiques and their requirements for entrants' participation, the *Directory of Seasonal/Holiday Craft Boutiques* can be ordered. Write for information about this directory (include a self-addressed stamped envelope) to:

The Front Room Publishers
P.O. Box 1541
Clifton, New Jersey 07015-1541.

QUESTIONS TO ASK:	Do my items have to be in seasonal colors? Who pays the return shipping on any unsold items? Does the boutique carry insurance on items during the show?

Selling on Consignment

A viable and often lucrative alternative to direct and wholesale sales is selling on consignment. Artists and craftspeople can place their work on consignment to galleries, shops, and other types of retail outlets (such as holiday boutiques), which simply means that they entrust their products to another to sell. A percentage of the selling price is then deducted for the service provided. The consignment arrangement benefits artisan and seller alike.

Photo: Dynamic Focus Photography
©1992

Consignment sales provide excellent outlets for beginning sellers' products. For the shop, consignments eliminate much of the financial risk of carrying works of unknown, questionable market appeal. If the work does not sell or sells poorly, the shop loses less money, because it has made no direct investment by purchasing the piece. The shop only loses use of the display space. In consignment selling, the artisan places merchandise in the care of the store owner, but receives no guarantee of sale.

Consignment provides an opportunity for the artisan to get a product into retail outlets where his items might not otherwise be readily accepted. For many unknown artists or craftspeople, consignment is the only means by which they can prove that their work will sell.

Kathy Wood, buyer for the gift shops at the Loews Anatole Hotel in Dallas, Texas, explains, "If we are not sure how an item will do sometimes, and if the company is small, we will ask them to do consignment. If it works real well, then we'll purchase from them, and if it doesn't, we return the merchandise and

3

nobody has had anything to lose." The Loews Anatole is willing to work with artists because they want things in their shops that are "different."

Although most items are sold to galleries, boutiques, and retail shops on consignment, other creative outlets exist. In Bellingham, Washington, twenty artists consigned their original work for the much anticipated opening of the Gardens of Art. Consigned works in the Gardens of Art range in price from fifty to several thousand dollars.

If an outlet accepts merchandise on consignment, an artist or craftsperson presents his or her work to the buyer, both parties specify a retail selling price, and they both sign a consignment agreement. The buyer gives a receipt for the work that lists the items accepted as well as selling prices. If and when the items sell, the gallery keeps a fixed percentage, usually around 50 percent of the selling price. This percentage should be decided ahead of time by both parties since it determines the retail selling price.

Consignment selling enables small shop owners with limited capital to conduct business more competitively. Such shops, in turn, provide local talent a start and furnish a good way to test prices and the marketability of a wide range of goods. For some artists, consignment is the only condition under which shop owners will take certain crafts, especially from unestablished craftspeople or those with expensive one-of-a-kind pieces. These items, by their very nature, are not highly marketable, so they place a financial burden on the shop owner. Upon sale of an item, craftspeople can earn more money than when selling at wholesale, and they retain ownership of the property until it is purchased by the consumer.

The disadvantages of selling by consignment include increased bookkeeping and paperwork for both shop owner and seller. For the latter, merchandise is tied up, but not sold, which can present cash-flow problems. The most common consignment hazards the seller faces center around the shop owners' lack of concern for goods they do not own; goods might be left to fade in sunny windows, become shop-worn, or simply lost due to shoplifting, breakage, or mishandling; sometimes new shops close suddenly and owners and stock disappear overnight; and others simply declare bankruptcy and creditors may have the right to seize consigned goods.

It is unwise to leave work at a shop without a written consignment

Wooden Rocking Horse
See related information in
Chapter 32
Photo: Dynamic Focus Photography
©1992

agreement signed by both parties. Shops usually have a standard agreement form, which lists the duration of consignment, describes each item in detail, and explains how merchandise is to be displayed and maintained. The selling price, the price the artist or craftsperson will be paid, and when payment will be made should be delineated. Any standard consignment contract should also contain the method of payment (monthly or immediately upon sale) and define the burden of responsibility in case of loss or damage. Always inquire whether the store's insurance policy covers consigned items.

These states have adopted consignment laws designed to protect artists and craftspeople: California, Colorado, Texas, Connecticut, Illinois, Massachusetts, New Mexico, New York, Oregon, Washington, and Wisconsin. Each state's laws provide different amounts of protection. State legislators' office personnel should be able to refer artisans to laws that would apply to consignment.

PLAN FOR SUCCESSFUL CONSIGNMENT SELLING

1. *Investigate the shops under consideration.* Learn how long the shop has existed, how well the business is established, and if the shop owner is sufficiently known in the community. Ask what type of merchandise is sold, how well other items carried by the shop relate to yours, and what type of clientele is attracted to the shop. Add any other questions that arise from your own experience.

2. *Avoid consignment to shops that buy most of their items.* Sometimes items are taken on consignment because buyers are unconvinced they will sell for one reason or another. For economic reasons, shops usually promote the items they have purchased first. Thus, they may not work as hard to help promote consigned merchandise.

3. *Consign only a few items at first.* Until a satisfactory rapport is developed with the owner or manager of a new or unknown shop, leave only a limited selection of your work. If prompt payment follows sales and if shop operations are well managed, then consign more products or items.

4. *Check on items at the shop.* Periodically inspect the items left on consignment. Shops may miss payments for items that have sold. If errors occur, alert

management without delay and follow up to see if the mistake is promptly corrected. Look at where, how, and/or if your pieces are being displayed.

5. *Never leave merchandise without a signed consignment agreement.* If not provided by the shop, standard consignment forms are available through other sources. The consignment agreement should include insurance coverage, pricing, commission, payment dates, how merchandise is to be displayed and maintained, and when unsold merchandise will be returned.

6. *Keep a running inventory.* Maintain an accurate record of all items delivered. Include the date and asking price. When each item is sold, indicate the amount received from the shop and date of receipt.

7. *Support the consignment outlet (shop, boutique, gallery).* Support all efforts of a good consignment outlet to sell your work. Never compete by selling the same items in places such as craft fairs for lower prices than the selling price of those items you have placed on consignment.

FOR ADDITIONAL INFORMATION ABOUT CONSIGNMENT SELLING

For a free booklet from the SBA: *Selling Products on Consignment* (No. 4.007), write:

U.S. Small Business Administration
Management Assistant Publications
P.O. Box 15434
Fort Worth, Texas 76119.

To order consignment agreements, write:
The Unicorn
Box 645
Rockville, Maryland 20851.

For more information and sample agreements, consult:
The Artist's Guide to the Art Market
by Betty Chamberlain
New York, Watson-Guptill Publications

The Artist's Survival Manual
    Toby Judith Klayman and Cobbett Steinberg
    New York: Charles Scribner's Sons

The Fine Artist's Guide to Showing and Selling Your Work
    Sally Prince Davis
    Cincinnati, Ohio: North Light Books

This Business of Art
    Diane Cochrane
    New York: Watson-Guptill Publications

Legal Guide for the Visual Artist
    Tad Crawford
    New York: Allworth Press

CHAPTER 2

Alternative Spaces

PRODUCTS BUYERS WANT: arts and crafts

COSTS TO CONSIDER: from $25

The alternative-space movement emerged as a reaction to the rigid structure found at many commercial galleries. Artists became innovative, and began organizing and developing their own exhibition spaces, using such places as abandoned factories. Indoor and outdoor public spaces that were not previously considered places to view or experience art became popular.

Most providers of alternative spaces not only furnish artists with exhibition facilities and moral support, but also invite experimentation. Their main intention is to aid artists who have not yet established connections with galleries. New exhibitors will be asked to comply with different mandates by the sponsoring organizations, but generally the managers of these places are much more receptive to off-beat ideas than are official institutions such as museums.

Selling work by utilizing unused space presents profitable opportunities. Many times artists are provided with a wonderful gallery-like setting for their creations, since artwork can be displayed wherever wall space is found. Popular places for exhibitions include banks, office buildings, hospitals, libraries, restaurants, parks, alleys, rooftops, and building facades. These are only a small sampling of alternative sites and spaces artists have employed as focal points, props, and backdrops for projects.

SPECIAL FEATURES: The alternative-space movement continues to grow, since this system provides areas for general exhibitions and performances, in addition to offering exhibition opportunities for particular artists. Alternative spaces have been dedicated to African American artists, female artists, Hispanic artists, artists born, raised, or living in specific neighborhoods of cities, and all minorities.

HOW TO CONTACT: Artists can locate exhibition places/spaces by contacting the following:

Information for Artists

CARO

183 Bathurst Street
Toronto, Ontario, Canada M5T 2R7.
Lists a variety of alternative avenues for exhibition and sale of works.

National Listings

National Association of Artists' Organizations Directory
918 F Street, N.W.
Washington, D.C. 20004.
Revised regularly, this publication describes alternative spaces and arts service organizations. Each entry includes a description of programs, disciplines, exhibition spaces, and proposal procedures, and provides the name of a contact person.

Art in America: Annual Guide to Galleries, Museums and Artists
Art in America
575 Broadway
New York, New York 10012.
An alphabetical listing published annually in the fall which contains a listing of alternative spaces in addition to museums and galleries, arranged by state

and city. Entries include the address, phone number, business hours, names of key staff members, and a description of art shown.

Regional Listings

Access: A Guide to the Visual Arts in Washington State
Allied Arts of Seattle
107 South Main
Seattle, Washington 98104.
Lists alternative and nonprofit spaces, commercial galleries, college and university galleries, museums, and percent-for-art agencies.

Washington Art: A Guide to Galleries, Art Consultants and Museums
Art Calendar
P.O. Box 1040
Great Falls, Virginia 22066.
Provides detailed profiles on alternative spaces, commercial galleries, art consultants, art centers, and museums in the Washington, D.C. area.

The Artists' Guide to Philadelphia
The Artists' Guide
P.O. Box 8755
Philadelphia, Pennsylvania 19101.
Profiles alternative spaces, commercial galleries, art centers, organizations, and resources in the Philadelphia area; each entry includes a description of facilities, price range, type of work exhibited, appointment procedures, and the name of a contact person.

Artists' Gallery Guide for Chicago and the Illinois Region
Chicago Artists' Coalition
5 West Grand
Chicago, Illinois 60610.
A guide to alternative and commercial galleries, museums, university galleries, and arts organizations in Chicago, north central and south central Illinois, southeast Wisconsin, St. Louis, Missouri, and northwest Indiana.

Marilyn Todd-Daniels
"Ring of Fire" (Mixed Media)
See related information in
Chapter 33

Public Hangings
    The City Gallery
    New York City Department of Cultural Affairs
    2 Columbus Circle
    New York, New York 10019.
    Lists more than eighty alternative spaces in New York City.

QUESTIONS TO ASK: How much does space cost?
Who provides the displays?
Are there special seasonal events planned that bring customers to the gallery?

CHAPTER 3

Architects

Discover an
Easy Means
to Sell
Arts and
Crafts to
Architects

PRODUCTS BUYERS WANT: crafts (architectural glass, lighting and neon, metal, stone, wood, ceramics, terra cotta, tiles, fiber, floor coverings, furniture and cabinetry)

COSTS TO CONSIDER: Call or write for latest price quotes.

Architectural Design Collaborators (A/DC) is an arts and crafts sourcebook for architects. The first edition of this comprehensive sourcebook for the architectural professions was published in 1990. *Architectual Design Collaborators* was then distributed free to principals of twenty thousand design firms with the American Institute of Architects and to every member of the Institute of Business Designers. Another four thousand copies were marketed to interior designers and real estate developers. The publication is endorsed by major organizations in the architectural field and professional design societies such as the International Association of Lighting Designers. Founder Malcolm Stevens established *Architectural Design Collaborators* (A/DC) to advance the Bauhaus ideal of collaboration between qualified artists and architects.

Entries are juried for possible participation in the sourcebook. Selected participants may then buy full-color or black-and-white pages to showcase their products or services. Judges include public art consultants along with other highly qualified individuals chosen from various design fields, such as graphic arts, environmental graphics, model making, industrial illustration, industrial design, and rendering.

SPECIAL FEATURE: An excellent way to reach thousands of architects, designers, and real estate developers seeking artists' work.

HOW TO CONTACT: **Resource World Publications**
209 West Central Street, Suite 204
Natick, Massachusetts 01760

QUESTIONS TO ASK: How do I acquire written information about this sourcebook?
What are the jurying rules?
How many artists from each craft category are included in the sourcebook?

CHAPTER 4

Museum Gift Shops

PRODUCTS BUYERS WANT: arts and crafts

COSTS TO CONSIDER: Samples submitted for consideration, telephone calls, and mailing costs. Figure on about $10 to $100.

In 1967, for the first time in the Metropolitan Museum of Art's history, there was a small gift shop installed near the entrance to the exhibition "In the Presence of Kings." Museum gift shops have proliferated ever since.

When searching for interesting gifts, people can escape the crowds and the ordinary by shopping museum gift shops. Unusual items await the unorthodox buyer at museums, from The Tattoo Art Museum in San Francisco to the Candy Americana Museum in Lititz, Pennsylvania. Stop along the way to visit three special museums in Eureka Springs, Arkansas—Geuther's Doll Museum, Miles Mountain Musical Museum, and the Bible Museum. There's the Barbed Wire Museum in LaCrosse, Kansas, and the American Museum of Magic in Marshall, Michigan.

For automobile aficionados, Towe Ford Museum located in Deer Lodge, Montana, has model Fords for every year from 1903 to 1952. If Chevrolets are preferred, then take a detour along the way to visit Chevyland U.S.A. in Elm Creek, Nebraska. Chevyland owners boast that they have the most complete collection of Chevrolets with all vehicles either original or restored and in running condition. Practically every museum has a gift shop that features a fantastic assortment of undiscovered treasures.

Museum gift shops such as the one located in Winterthur, Delaware, have become so popular with gift-buying customers that they are now opening shops located outside their original museum location. A Winterthur Museum Gift Shop, which offers an extraordinary selection of unusual items, is located in Alexandria, Virginia. The shop's stock is complete with an outdoor garden featuring two pet squirrels that the manager jokingly said, "run too fast to be tagged with prices—unfortunately."

SPECIAL FEATURE: Most museum gift shops accept charge cards, making it easier for shoppers to spend large amounts of money in these treasure-troves.

....

QUESTIONS TO ASK:　Do you purchase work wholesale or take work on consignment?
Will you return my sample(s) insured?
If work is consigned to the shop, what is my percentage?

....

MUSEUM GIFT SHOPS EAGER TO SEE ARTISAN'S WORK

Downey Museum of Art
10419 Rives Avenue
Downey, California 90241
(310) 861-0419
All types of crafts; submit slides, descriptions, prices, SASE.

Delaware Art Museum
2301 Kentmere Parkway
Wilmington, Delaware 19806
(302) 571-9590
Fiber, metal, wood, ceramic, paper, plastic items with modern, upscale or funky look; retail to $150; frequent exhibitions; submit slides/photos, descriptions, prices, SASE.

Museum of Art/Museum Store

One East Las Olas Boulevard
Fort Lauderdale, Florida 33301
(305) 525-5500
Pottery, glass, porcelain, jewelry, dolls, woodcrafted toys; retail to $125; frequent exhibitions; submit slides/photos, descriptions, prices, SASE.

The Contemporary Museum Shop

2411 Makiki Heights Drive
Honolulu, Hawaii 96822
(808) 523-3447
Fine, unusual, contemporary jewelry, glass, ceramics, wood sculpture; retail price range open; two to three exhibitions per year; submit slides/photos, descriptions, prices, SASE.

Lakeview Museum Shop and Sales/Rental Gallery

1125 West Lake Avenue
Peoria, Illinois 61614
(309) 686-7000
Jewelry, wood, glass; retail to $150; frequent exhibitions; submit slides/photos, descriptions, prices, SASE.

Columbus Museum Shop

372 Commons Mall
Columbus, Indiana 47201
(812) 376-2559
All crafts; retail to $400; frequent exhibitions planned; submit photos, descriptions, prices, SASE.

The Indiana State Museum Shop

202 North Alabama
Indianapolis, Indiana 46204
(317) 632-5007
All crafts from Indiana; retail to $100; frequent exhibitions; submit descriptions, prices, SASE.

Christiane Schwarcz
Barrette in Brass with Copper Triangles
See related information in Chapter 32
Photo: Dynamic Focus Photography
©1993

17

Guild Hall Museum Shop
158 Main Street
East Hampton, New York 11937
(516) 324-0806
Retail price range open; eight exhibitions per year; submit photos, descriptions, prices, SASE.

Johnstown Flood Museum Gift Shop
P.O. Box 1889
Johnstown, Pennsylvania 15907
(814) 539-1889
Traditional and ethnic crafts; beadwork, embroidery, weaving, wood carving, paper cutting; retail to $100; submit photos/slides, prices, SASE.

Museum Store—Oklahoma City Art Museum
3113 Pershing Boulevard
Oklahoma City, Oklahoma 73107
(405) 946-4477
Interested in jewelry, glass, porcelain, ceramic items, greeting cards; retail to $100; consignment only; submit photos, descriptions, prices, SASE.

Museum of Appalachia Gift Shop
P.O. Box 0318
Norris, Tennessee 37828
(615) 494-7325 or (615) 494-0514
All crafts; retail $1 to $500; submit photos, descriptions, prices, SASE.

Bellevue Art Museum Gift Shop
301 Bellevue Square
Bellevue, Washington 98004
(206) 454-3322
All crafts; retail to $800; six exhibitions per year; submit descriptions, prices, SASE.

National Museum of Women in the Arts Gift Shop
1250 New York Avenue, N.W.
Washington, D.C. 20005-3920
(202) 783-5000
Interested in jewelry, beadwork, leather; submit samples, prices.

....

MAILING LISTS WITH MUSEUM GIFT SHOPS

For a mailing list containing the names and addresses of 530 art museum bookstore buyers ($65):
ArtNetwork
13284 Rices Crossing Road
P.O. Box 369
Renaissance, California 95962-0369
(800) 383-0677 or fax (916) 692-1370

For a mailing list of 320 museum shops and stores ($40):
Visual Studies
49 Rivoli Street
San Francisco, California 94117

In addition, The Museum Store Association is an organization for museum shop buyers. Membership in this association can aid sales efforts to the museum shop market.
Museum Store Association
501 South Cherry Street
Suite 460
Denver, Colorado 80222
(303) 329-6968

Wooden Apples
Photo: Americraft Gift Brokers

CHAPTER 5

A Crafts Broker

Try a New Idea by Selling Your Work through a Crafts Broker

PRODUCTS BUYERS WANT: Crafts (especially those items that are unusual or extra special). You must have minimum production of $1,000 per week. If qualified, send your brochure to Americraft Gift Brokers for a free consultation.

COSTS TO CONSIDER: Americraft charges a commission of about 20 percent on each sale. No commissions are paid until a sale is made and payment is received.

"What Americraft does is prescreen products for the entire mail order industry, so if anybody's got anything that's got a prayer of selling in catalogs, we can direct it to the appropriate buyers," Director Bob Cabral said. "We do a degree of coaching at that stage in terms of grooming them (crafters) for presentation and going over production capabilities."

When selecting work to broker, Americraft Gift Brokers looks for quality design and execution, good value, and most important, realistic production schedules. Since they began, Cabral has emphasized test marketing new ideas without needless investment. "We are really only geared toward people who have done well and tested products at retail crafts shows and are looking to get into real volume wholesaling. Our definition of that is a minimum production of $1,000 a week."

Cabral believes that, "The key thing in making products sell for catalogs is they have to have a different spin. Even for people who are already doing well at retail crafts shows, people who have mastered a given media, they need that extra little oomph."

One of the ways Cabral tries to communicate this indefinable attribute to clients is to ask them if they ever come into their facilities on off-time over the weekend to use the equipment to make something special for a close family member. By doing this, crafters have created some innovative products that differ from their regular line. Cabral emphasizes, "That's how the best products get developed."

They have a number of items that are selling well nationally that came out of weekend ideas. "Like when I was out in the woods, I was whittling my girlfriend's and my name into a tree and I thought, 'How can I automate this?' and a way of doing it flashed into my head. All of a sudden I am whittling two names into an apple and it looks just exactly like it's hand-carved..." That apple has been selling really well through catalogs such as *Casual Living* and *Colorful Images* for over two years.

Bob Cabral started out years ago with a shop in Nantucket, Massachusetts. Then he learned that marketing effectively through catalogs was possible from remote places like an island. "Consequently, I have filled a need, because I couldn't find anyone to take my work and get it to all these catalogs, so I created the databases and basically the electronic marketing system that allows us to effectively get ideas to the buyers."

Americraft maintains a library of product brochures along with all sorts of craft samples. When they learn of a sales opportunity, they then send the buyer a packet of brochures representing a good mix of appropriate crafts. If the buyer requests samples, Americraft responds immediately. Their marketing method has elicited a steady stream of purchase orders since 1978 from stores such as Neiman Marcus, The Horchow Collection, L.L. Bean, Eddie Bauer, Casual Living, David Kay, Lands End, and even Orvis, the oldest catalog house in the country.

Ceramic Cat Clock
Photo: Americraft Gift Brokers

Another significant marketing tool is their in-house mailing list of specialty shops. The museum store market has also been good. Americraft Gift Brokers works hard to maintain its well-established reputation with the catalog buyers who know that if Bob Cabral refers a craft product then it merits serious consideration.

SPECIAL FEATURES: Americraft's brokering concept consists of knowledgeable product screening, coupled with specific target marketing. By utilizing Americraft's methods, catalog buyers never waste time wading through unnecessary promotional materials, and craft producers save marketing dollars. Craft brokering offers marketing contacts that allow industrious craftspeople a gateway into diverse markets which are normally prohibitively expensive to individuals.

Wooden Stick Pens
Photo: Americraft Gift Brokers

HOW TO CONTACT:

Details available from
Americraft Gift Brokers
  P.O. Box 814
  Wendell, Massachusetts 01379
  (800) 866-CRAFT, (508) 544-7330
  or fax (508) 544-2771

QUESTIONS TO ASK:

What type of promotional materials do I have to furnish?
How many samples are usually required?
Do you need slides?

Kali Bradford
"Dreamers" (Sand)
Photo: Kali Bradford

CHAPTER 6

Selling Through a Garden

PRODUCTS BUYERS WANT: arts and crafts for the garden

COSTS TO CONSIDER: consignment percentage

Gardens of Art is located in northern Washington State near the Canadian border and the Pacific coast. George Drake, originator of the garden, says, "Within an hour-and-a-half drive we have over six million people." Gardens of Art is about a mile off the highway. Kali Bradford, the new manager of Gardens of Art, now designated as a city park, is busy adding art to her medium of sand sculpture. Her legendary mega-ton sand castles are already adding a new dimension to the garden's landscape.

One hundred varieties of Japanese maples and other east-Asian plants flanked by Oregon grape and huckleberry bushes sit on this two-and-a-half-acre hilltop garden. In the spring, the unique azaleas and rhododendrons in bloom provide a magnificent backdrop for the artists' consigned works.

"I had many people from other parts of the world and certainly other parts of the nation saying it was a world-class presentation. We had over $2 million in inventory in art. We had incredible bronzes from Bill Epp, who is one of the most famous Canadian sculptors," says George Drake.

More than one hundred works by twenty-five sculptors are displayed. Their diverse sculptures have included an eclectic selection such as ceramic fountains,

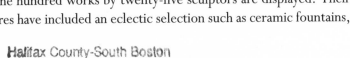

a fused-glass piece titled *Glass Rounds*, and a geometric aluminum sculpture called *The Cube*. Some of the stoneware has been on display out in the garden for over fifteen years. Drake says, "The point is that the work has to be done for outdoor showing."

The artists' works range in price from $50 to several thousand dollars. Although most of the artwork is in the $1,000 to $10,000 price range, the price tag on H. A. Fadhli's metal sculpture, entitled *Timeless*, of a mare and newborn foal lying on a bed of straw, is $35,000.

There seem to be lots of collectors who can afford the art displayed in Gardens of Art. Since the garden's grand opening in 1988, they have had a successful operation. George Drake's initial assertion that "there is an incredible market for garden art that is well done!" has proved to be prophetic.

SPECIAL FEATURE: Work that is submitted must be for outdoor showing only. The Gardens of Art is open to visitors from May 1 to October 30.

HOW TO CONTACT: Gardens of Art administrators are looking for artisans interested in showing work at the garden. Write for more information to:
Gardens of Art
2900 Sylvan Street
Bellingham, Washington 98226
or telephone (206) 671-1069

QUESTIONS TO ASK: Will you accept my piece if sent by mail?
How much is your consignment percentage?
How many artists' works are represented in the garden?

Originator of Gardens of Art

"My wife and I started a beautiful garden within two-and-a-half acres of woods on a hilltop with views in all directions," originator George Drake said. "We created that to provide a climate for handicapped people, including our son, who has Down's syndrome. It was a commercial nursery as well as a garden. Then about eight years ago I started showing fine arts for the garden worth up to $50,000. We were moving multi-thousands of dollars' worth of art there. Then the city bought the property for a park and leased out the concession for selling art."

Many avid art collectors' homes are so filled with art that if they're going to keep on buying they need another place for display. So they usually decide to begin placing art objects outside in their garden. This opens up another colossal market for enterprising artisans. Drake has the following advice for artists who want to consider providing art for gardens:

■ *Consider the weather.* "All pieces have to be impervious to the weather because they are all shown outdoors. When art is prepared for showing in the garden, the artist has to think about the impact of weather." For instance, are the dyes that have been used in the piece sensitive to sunlight? Sometimes after a year of exposure, the color just fades into nothing. Do not run the risk of an irate customer who paid $2,000 for a piece coming back and saying, "You said I could put this in the garden and it's now mush." The artist, as a technician, should know about every product used. "I had an artist send me a fused-glass piece. I didn't realize that certain parts they glued instead of fusing, and the rain melted the glue. It literally fell apart on me! Don't risk your reputation as an artist, along with the (gallery) owner's reputation by giving them work like that. I've had beautiful stoneware out there for up to fifteen years, stoneware pieces that are the size of a kitchen chair, done by Clayton James, who is now in his seventies. The point is that the work has to be done for outdoor showing. One has to be sensitive to the play of weather on your pieces."

■ *Be open-minded.* Think about other display possibilities for your art. Gardens can provide a perfect showcase. Drake admits, "It was a job trying to make artists aware that their work would be appropriate for the outdoors if they would only adjust this or that." However, artists must think through the display process. "You can't put iron wire for hanging a plate and expect it not to (eventually) rust and break." Two-dimensional pieces can often be hung. "We've had some beautiful tile plates and plaques for the wall, enameled copper paintings that we seal in a frame and put on the wall."

Art Hohl
"Star Hunters I"

■ *Think about safety.* Drake received a sculpture that stood five feet tall and weighed two hundred pounds, on a footprint that was only about six inches wide with no way to secure the piece. "I don't know what they think I'm going to do with it. Sure, I can balance it. But can you imagine a five-year-old child pushing that thing over? You really have to think about safety." Drake has had to ask another artist to remove a mobile with pointed steel spikes that when swinging in the wind could have pierced through someone. "I didn't want to take the risk."

■ *Try to remember that gallery owners are small businesses, too, trying to survive.* "Galleries have to survive or artists aren't going to have any place to sell their work." Be realistic when considering the various business aspects, such as the amount of insurance required. "It takes years to build up a reputation. It's going to have to be a cooperative relationship, one based on trust."

■ *Provide special instructions to the buyer.* For example, does the artwork need to be waxed? If so, how often and when? It should not be assumed that the buyer of art knows such details.

"I put a little one-sentence ad in two popular gardening magazines—*American Horticulture* and *Flower and Garden*. It said FREE. One-year subscription to *Garden Art*, a newsletter for fine arts for the garden." Within one month he had six thousand inquiries. "There's a market throughout America for fine art for the garden." Drake says that he knows from personal experience that the better artists are not even aware of the potential of this huge market. He feels that one way they can reach it is go to the finest nurseries, the ones that sell $1,000 trees. Talk to the owner or manager and say, "Here's some quality material."

Drake maintains that there's a growing market for garden art. Some pieces cost as much as $20,000. In fact, Drake said, "My last year I sold a quarter of a million dollars of fine art for the garden."

"We started this garden, this beautiful garden, to provide employment for the brain-damaged, mentally retarded, and mentally ill." Drake is now beginning a new project, one which involves using garden art as therapy. He is funding the Horticultural Therapy Committee for the development of a program of horticultural therapy at Big Rock Garden Park. "The newest population are the Alzheimer's victims. It has been found that the Alzheimer's victims can concentrate longer periods of time on gardening activities than anything else." They get involved in all areas such as maintaining the paths and walkways. Drake sighs, "It's come full circle and we feel really good about it."

Warren Arnold
Warren Arnold Marble Figure

Phillip Argent
University of Nevada Las Vegas
"Airspace" (Acrylic and Collage
on Canvas)
See related information in
Chapter 38
Courtesy of: Binney and Smith, Inc.
University Student Grant Program

CHAPTER 7

Corporate Art Markets

PRODUCTS BUYERS WANT:	fine arts and museum-quality crafts
COSTS TO CONSIDER:	a minimum of $5 for long-distance telephone charges or shipping

*Prosperity
Through
Today's Patrons
of the Arts*

In the past, art commissions originated from kings of countries and the church. Today, corporations act as the latest patron saints of the arts. The corporate art market includes a wide range of institutions, running the gamut from private enclaves like financial corporations and law offices to places with more public exposure, such as hospitals and restaurants. Corporations exhibit collections in the offices of many companies, at banks, and even in shopping malls. More than one thousand major corporations, including Atlantic Richfield, AT&T, and IBM purchase all types of art. Additionally, thousands of midsize and small companies collect art.

Businesses actively search for appropriate pieces that suit their company's image. Purchasers of corporate art say their reason for assembling an art collection is to improve the working environment for employees. Some art acquisitions relate directly to the company's specialty. The Kohler Company of Kohler, Wisconsin, a manufacturer of plumbing fixtures, collects ceramic art. Borg-Warner, located in Chicago, Illinois, selects works by contemporary artists who live within a 250-mile radius, thus effectively establishing strong civic ties to talented regional artists. Chase Manhattan Bank's corporate art collection is one of the largest in this country. Chase displays more than twelve thousand separate paintings, textiles, photographs, prints, pieces of folk art, and sculpture, by emerging American artists.

SPECIAL FEATURE: *USA Today* quotes the editor of *Interiors Magazine*, Beverly Russell: "Companies will begin supporting American craftspeople to create unique pieces of furniture…for dining rooms, lobbies, offices. These will be the antiques of the future."

HOW TO CONTACT: Artists should contact the art director, public relations director, or corporate communications director who is in charge of buying art for the particular company. After the conversation is concluded, a promotional package consisting of a cover letter, resumé, slides, and a self-addressed stamped envelope (SASE) should be promptly mailed to the persons to whom you spoke. Names and addresses of many corporate curators are listed in the following:

The International Directory of Corporate Art Collections

ARTnews
48 West 38th Street
New York, New York 10018

Directory of Fine Art Representatives and Corporate Art Collections

ArtNetwork
P.O. Box 369
13284 Rices Crossing Road
Renaissance, California 95962

Art in America Annual Guide to Galleries, Museums, and Artists

Art in America
575 Broadway
New York, New York 10012

The ARTnews Directory of Corporate Art Collections lists six hundred corporations that collect art. This directory notes the names of corporate curators, themes, and other relevant information such as descriptions of the collections. For information, write:

ARTnews Directory of Corporate Art Collections
5 West 37th Street
New York, New York 10018

Customized mailing lists provide names and addresses of seven hundred corporations that collect art and are large-scale purchasers of both originals and prints. A list of two hundred fifty corporations that collect photography is also available. Both can be purchased for one-time usage from:

ArtNetwork
13284 Rices Crossing Road
P.O. Box 369
Renaissance, California 95962-0369
(800) 383-0677

K.L. Tafoya
"Into the Wind" (Oil on Linen)
See related information in
Chapter 33

For a listing of the particulars concerning the artistic interests of corporations, subsidiaries, affiliates and the officers involved, consult:

National Directory of Arts and Education Support by Business Corporations (available in some libraries):

Washington International Arts Letter
P.O. Box 9005
Washington, D.C. 20003

Can you send me information?
How often and when are your lists updated?
Does it cost to be listed?

QUESTIONS TO ASK:

CORPORATE CONTRACTS:

Selling art to corporations presents stimulating new opportunities for artists and craftspeople willing to cope with rigorous rules. Often corporations request time-consuming activities such as frequent professional presentations, rigid adherence to schedules, and willingness to collaborate. In order to avoid potential problems, crafters and artists should establish agreed-upon conditions, and put expectations in writing as much and as soon as possible.

The commission contract is an essential component of the corporate art world. The contract functions to reduce the risk of misunderstanding the intentions of each party. A well-drawn contract specifies procedures for resolving conflicts and provides tangible evidence for enforcing the agreement in court.

ART-BUYING CORPORATIONS IN THE UNITED STATES

1. *Chase Manhattan Bank displays artwork in the bank's offices around the world.* Chase constantly buys artistic pieces for its collection which includes paintings, original works on paper, prints, sculpture, photographs, folk art, and textiles. Its displays are changed frequently. Chase will look at any artist's resumé, brochure, and sheet of slides. Contact:

Chase Manhattan Bank
Art Program Manager
One Chase Manhattan Plaza
New York, New York 10081
(212) 552-2222

2. *The Kemper Group's collection is displayed throughout the halls and work areas of the home office.* The group will give consideration to all media, including oils, acrylics, watercolors, original graphics, drawings, photography, and sculpture from Chicago and midwestern artists. Contact:

Kemper Group
Curator
1 Kemper Drive
Long Grove, Illinois 60049
(708) 540-2502

3. *Atlantic Richfield Company displays its ongoing collection throughout its fifty buildings across the country.* It strives to support community arts in cities where its offices are located. The ARCO collection includes: works on paper, paintings, sculpture, textiles, and photography. Artists should submit an introductory letter, a resumé, and slides. Samples will be filed for future referral. Contact:

Atlantic Richfield Company
Project Coordinator
515 South Flower Street
Los Angeles, California 90071
(213) 486-8666

4. *First Banks of Minneapolis shows off works of art they purchase from regional artists in private offices, reception areas, and lobbies.* They are looking for paintings, sculpture, works on paper, mixed media, photography and crafts done in oils, acrylics, watercolor, pastels, pen-and-ink, collage, and glass. Artists should send slides and appropriate written information, including a biography, artist statement, critical reviews, and a list of exhibitions. Contact:

First Banks of Minneapolis,
Curator
601 Second Avenue South
Minneapolis, Minnesota 55402
(612) 973-4004

5. *Borg-Warner exhibits all types of media in a variety of styles, from realism to abstraction, by artists in the Chicago area.* Artists should send slides documenting medium, size, year completed, and price, along with biographical information with an SASE. Contact:

Borg-Warner,
Curator
200 South Michigan Avenue
Chicago, Illinois 60604
(312) 322-8500

6. *The Amoco Corporation has been assembling works since 1972.* Its collection, primarily composed of contemporary graphics, is displayed throughout the Chicago headquarters. It needs a resumé and slides. Contact:

Amoco Corporation,
Curator
Arts Collection
200 East Randolph Drive
Chicago, Illinois 60601
(312) 856-2701

7. *The Hospital Corporation of America's collection focuses on works by emerging, contemporary artists in Nashville, Tennessee.* Its acquisitions include sculpture, photographs, mixed media, and experimental works on paper by sculptors and constructionists. Contact:

Hospital Corporation of America
Arts Administrator
One Park Plaza
Nashville, Tennessee 37203
(615) 327-9551

ADDITIONAL CORPORATIONS THAT ARE INTERESTED IN COLLECTING ART

Brunswick Corporation
One Brunswick Plaza
Skokie, Illinois 60076

Celanese Corporation
1211 Avenue of the Americas
New York, New York 10036

Citicorp
399 Park Avenue
New York, New York 10022

Continental Bank Foundation
231 South LaSalle Street
Chicago, Illinois 60693

Equitable Life Assurance Society
1285 Avenue of the Americas
New York, New York 10019

Gulf and Western Co., Inc.
One Gulf and Western Plaza
New York, New York 10023

Gulf Oil Foundation
P.O. Box 1166
Pittsburgh, Pennsylvania 15230

Houston Natural Gas Corporation
P.O. Box 1188
Houston, Texas 77001

International Business Machines Corporation
Old Orchard Road
Armonk, New York 10504

Kimberly-Clark
401 North Lake Street
Neenah, Wisconsin 54956

Lever Brothers Company, Inc.
390 Park Avenue
New York, New York 10022

Mobil Oil Company
150 East 42nd Street
New York, New York 10017

Polaroid Foundation, Inc.
750 Main Street
Cambridge, Massachusetts 02139

The Quaker Oats Foundation
345 Merchandise Mart
Chicago, Illinois 60654

Xerox Corporation
800 Long Ridge Road
P.O. Box 1600
Stamford, Connecticut 06904

FOR ADDITIONAL LEADS

Business Committee for the Arts, Inc.
1775 Broadway
New York, New York 10019

BOOKS

A Guide to Corporate Giving in the Arts
Bob Porter
American Council for the Arts, Department 43
One East 53rd Street
New York, New York 10022

CHAPTER 8

A Referral Service

*Making
Connections
with a Referral
Service*

SERVICE BUYERS WANT: for historic stained or fused-glass restoration craftspeople

---

COSTS TO CONSIDER: furnished upon request

Since 1987, McKernan Satterlee Associates, Inc., a consulting firm, has created a nationwide referral service for historic stained-glass restoration. These referrals help stained-glass craftspeople locate historic glass restoration work. Arrangements are made for restoration work to be performed on stained-glass windows of all types of structures ranging from churches to public/government buildings.

Julie L. Sloan, president of McKernan Satterlee Associates, says, "My master's degree is in historic preservation from Columbia; my bachelor's degree is in art history from NYU (New York University). As an art historian studying medieval art, I realized that stained-glass conservation was not something that the preservation world paid much attention. Although in Europe there were very sophisticated approaches to it, there weren't any here in the United States. So I did my thesis research on the conservation of stained glass in America. Basically that reinforced my feeling that it wasn't being treated as a serious art form, nor even as a serious architectural element. At the same time I was attending Columbia, in Brooklyn, a major stained-glass restoration project began under the auspices of New York Landmarks Conservancy. I did an internship with the Conservancy in the administration of that project.

"When I graduated from Columbia I went to the studio that was doing the work to do an apprenticeship. Then I left the studio to start my own company because it became more and more clear to me that owners needed a representative. They needed somebody to translate the language of stained-glass preservation for them. They needed a liaison because stained glass is such a mysterious field. So many people think this is a lost art. They really had no way of knowing whether their windows needed work, how much work they needed, whether the prices they were getting and the proposals they were getting were what their windows really needed."

Jobs have been located from California to New York, with some projects as far south as Kentucky. Work was performed on the windows in Trinity Church in Boston for three years. Their biggest project was Memorial Hall at Harvard University, which took one studio five years to complete. Sloan describes one of her company's "most stellar" projects to date as Frank Lloyd Wright's Robie House in Chicago.

Craftsworkers who are interested in restoration should submit a resumé, letter of recommendation, promotional material, and photographs of their best work. Interviews will be conducted over the telephone to determine mutual project interests. Work assignments are made based on the scope of the project with consideration given to the needs, requirements, and qualifications of the applicants.

SPECIAL FEATURES: Historic stained or fused-glass restoration projects and craftspeople can be located anywhere in the world. Applications of qualified workers are kept on file along with information about their studios so recommendations can be made by specialty or location. Listings are updated on an annual basis.

Details available from:
McKernan Satterlee Associates
  28 Sandlewood Road
  Newark, Delaware 19713
  (302) 738-2285

HOW TO CONTACT:

What kinds of photographs and promotional materials would you like to see?
How is the work arranged?

QUESTIONS TO ASK:

Debra Korluka
"Curly Stallion"
See related information in
Chapter 33

CHAPTER 9

Builders

PRODUCTS BUYERS WANT: arts and crafts work for homes or offices

---

COSTS TO CONSIDER: Associate membership dues start from $100 annually.

Home builder associations are an often overlooked marketing possibility for artisans today. These associations are filled not only with the builders who construct the spaces in which we live, but also with most of the subcontractors with whom they do business, as well as mortgage brokers, real estate agents, and many other potential customers for craftspeople.

"Five years ago it was the exception to the rule to see stained glass put in new home construction. Now you can't build competitively without it," says Dan Oppenheimer, who started Rainbow Studio/Stained Glass in 1973. Most often the builders determine what goes into new residential construction. Builders sign the purchase orders for amenities being built in, such as custom tiles, marble, wrought iron, and other hand-crafted products.

Though contacting builders directly can work, craftsworkers can build up credibility just by joining an association. Most builders pay much more attention to a subcontractor, which is how they view a craftsperson after you belong to their "club." Attendance at meetings and participation on committees that involve a builder or two can be critical to achieving success as an artisan.

SPECIAL FEATURE: This is a great way to reach a market, promote work, and interact with those who buy products. The National Association of Home Builders has 157,000 active members.

HOW TO CONTACT:

For information, contact:
National Association of Home Builders
15th and M Streets, N.W.
Washington, D.C. 20005
(202) 822-0200
Publishes *Nation's Building News* (accepts advertising)

QUESTIONS TO ASK:

What is the name, address, and telephone number of the home builder's association located in my area?
Could you please send me a free catalog?

Commissioned Work

A commissioned work refers to an art object that a client has paid an artisan to create—in other words, artwork made to order. Arrangements for this type of work by special order occur frequently. For example, Security National Bank in Texas wanted artwork that was reminiscent of "old" Arlington, so after examining more than three hundred photos that spanned five generations, it commissioned Dr. Marilyn Todd-Daniels to provide three paintings which are color replicas of actual photographs. Many hotels actively seek artisans' work. Liz Kregloe of Roanoke, Virginia, has handmade paper wall pieces hanging in the lobbies of four Marriott Hotel Residence Inns located in Pennsylvania, Maryland, New York, and California. Elizabeth Lewis Scott from Hartselle, Alabama, whose paintings have been purchased by the Kentucky Derby Museum, produces commissions that focus on capturing on canvas the special relationship between people and their horses.

Commissioned works are normally contractual sales opportunities where clients request that a specific work of art be created for their purchase. South Carolina fiber artist Ellen Kochansky created a twelve-foot-by-twelve-foot, quilted wall hanging titled *Winter*, one of four season-motif wall hangings commissioned by the architect, now showcased in the Chemed Center lobby in Cincinnati.

In addition to the money, commissioned works enhance an artist's reputation. The execution of a public sculpture, mural, or portrait of a prominent person

45

always augments an artist's credentials. When visitors enter the Lobby Bar of Atrium I in the Loews Anatole Hotel in Dallas, they immediately notice a fifteen-foot-high acrylic sculpture designed to appear as if it is constructed of ice, titled *Galatea* by Mike Cunningham of Denton, Texas. If they want to learn more about the artwork displayed in the hotel, the staff gladly distributes a free pamphlet titled *Anatole Art*.

Some commissions are granted on the basis of competitions. Remember, though, art competitions are as unpredictable as any other contest. Oftentimes jurors have a specific idea of the type work they want to choose, so the artist should not take offense if not chosen.

The word "commission" might refer to a client who seeks out the artist, which is often the case. But if the idea of assigned work is appealing, the artisan can take the first step by investigating potential markets. If, for example, an artist does detailed drawings of birds or flowers, they could seek information about upcoming commissions from natural history, bird, or botanical societies. They can also check announcements in art magazines that list when clients such as architects, designers, and arts councils make awards and sponsor competitions. For example, an issue of *American Artist* announced a sculpture competition, a juried show for women artists, and scholarships for midwestern artists.

If an artisan specializes in one area, such as dogs, then a search should be undertaken to find service businesses associated with this interest. In this case the target markets would be veterinarians, kennels, pet shops, and any other organizations whose focus is dogs. One enterprising pet artist travels the gunshow circuit setting up her booth next to gun, holster, and ammunition sellers. All she needs to paint a beloved pet's portrait on broken marble slabs is a reasonably clear photograph.

For information on numerous associations, check the *Encyclopedia of Associations*, available in most libraries. This multivolume reference work contains comprehensive listings of approximately twenty thousand national organizations. The organizations are indexed alphabetically by name and key word, such as "dog" (area of interest). The encyclopedia also includes separate indexes of geographic locations and the names and addresses of each association's chief executives.

Other sources for work include public institutions, private individuals, government grants, and corporations. When government agencies commission public artwork, often the agency tells the artist how much money is available for the project. The artist must see if he can work within that budget; in other words, the client quotes the price. But in most other cases, artists will be asked to give clients their price.

One fascinating type of government art commission is for the design of postage stamps. Acceptance is decided by the Citizens' Stamp Advisory Committee. This group pays approximately $1,500 per commission. Some years ago Robert Indiana's rendering of *"LOVE"* was accepted for a stamp. This committee of eleven also keeps a talent-bank file of resumés for future reference. Any artist can submit a resumé and slides for consideration by the group by writing the Chairman, Citizens' Stamp Advisory Committee, c/o Postmaster General, 475 L'Enfant Plaza W. SW., Room 5700, Washington, D.C. 20260. Usually, the committee does not actively seek design suggestions since they already maintain approximately four thousand subjects as backlog. They choose subjects, then select artists whose talent-bank file records indicate suitability for the commission.

Other organizations actively help artists obtain work on commission. The National Sculpture Society, 1177 Avenue of the Americas, New York, New York 10036, holds special competitions for and exhibitions of architectural sculpture. This society accepts work by nonmembers for some of its shows. The Architectural League of New York puts on frequent shows at the American Federation of Arts building located at 41 East 65th Street. The work displayed usually relates to subway-station design and city architectural planning. Portraits, Inc., 985 Park Avenue, New York, New York 10028, is a gallery with a roster of artists specializing in portrait painting. This gallery also acts as an agent for mural commissions. Look for commission opportunities offered through other guilds, associations, and artists' organizations.

Although commissioned works are a welcome addition to an artist's income, they are not without potential pitfalls. When creating such works, artisans do not simply work with personal aesthetic needs and desires; they are also working to meet the specified desires of the client. Avoid misunderstandings by signing a comprehensive written agreement with clients. When commissioned to create a work, artisans must make sure that the client has enough familiarity with their style, then they must be absolutely certain to have a detailed contract that addresses:

1. *Description of project.* Provides a detailed description of the commissioned work (dimensions, materials, construction methods). The artists should provide as many details as possible about their artwork to protect themselves. This description needs to be as accurate and complete as possible.

2. *Scheduling.* All important dates, such as the date that the project begins, the completion date and the delivery date, need to be specified. When the project is completed, a receipt should be requested. The client's satisfaction and acceptance ought to be noted.

3. *Payment plan.* An advance on the project provides the artisan with assurance of the buyer's intent. Typically, the client gives the artist half of the fee upon signing the contract, and the other half upon completing the project.

4. *Copyright.* All work should be copyrighted in the artisan's name. If the client wants reproduction rights, a higher price for his work is warranted.

5. *Other rights.* The contract should declare that the buyer cannot knowingly alter, change, modify, damage, or destroy the artwork. The contract's wording must provide that the client is responsible for providing for the safety and well-being of the work purchased.

6. *Termination of contract.* The contract should state exactly how the agreement can be canceled by either party. The contract should also declare that the client must provide reasonable cause in order to cancel the work.

7. *Originality of work.* The artisan should assure the buyer that the commissioned work is the original product of his creative efforts and that it is an edition of one.

There will not be one commission, one gallery, one award, or one show that "makes an artist's career." Instead, artistic careers are built on a series of commissions, sales, awards, and exhibitions, each adding to and complementing the others. Financial status will probably increase as reputation grows, but an artist's future depends on continued dedication, not an overnight windfall. As each achievement arrives, carefully lay the groundwork through marketing and self-promotion to ensure a successful future.

Courtney Miller and Lee
Peterson
"Formal Tom/Glamour Puss"
(Sterling Silver, Brass, Copper,
and Opal Companion Brooches)
See related information in
Chapter 20
Featured in Crafts Report's
Craft Showcase
*Photo: Crocker Studio, Inc.
Photography*
©1993

Rep Registry

....

PRODUCTS BUYERS WANT: arts and crafts

....

COSTS TO CONSIDER: registration fee: $35.
rep referral fee: $140.

....

*One Good
Way to Find
a Sales
Representative*

"We have more than four thousand reps currently registered with us," says Jill Ford of the Rep Registry, a placement service matching craftspersons and sale representatives. She created this referral service to help craftsworkers locate the best rep for the job. "We prescreen to make a marriage," Ford explains. "We don't take on a line unless we think we can find reps for them. We tell them (craftspeople), 'Work these two or three reps for a season or cycle. Then all you have to do is pick up the phone, call us, and say my cash flow is up; I'm ready to expand and take that next step. Hey Jill, find me a couple more reps,' and that's all they need to do. The longer we work with them the better we are able to pinpoint the kinds of reps they like, because we know who they've hired and who they're working well with."

Sales reps service the general gift market where the product can be sold over and over and over again. "We suggest they hire two or three reps," Ford says. "This way they get a good general picture of whether their product is, A) saleable, and B) saleable through reps.

"First, you fill out a registration form for us." The registration form consists of a checklist asking the following questions, which crafters who are interested in sales representatives should be thinking about and asking themselves:

- *What territories are you looking for?*

- *What type of retail stores are you currently selling to?*

- *What class of trade are you selling to (i.e., owner-operated, department store, chain stores)?*

- *How many salespeople do you currently employ?*

- *What type of sales support (such as brochures, wholesale price sheets, and samples) is provided?*

- *Are you currently exhibiting at trade shows?*

- *Do you require permanent showroom availability?*

- *Do you prefer a larger or smaller sales-rep organization?*

- *Who are some of your top-producing reps or rep firms?*

- *If you are replacing reps, who are you replacing and why?* What is the reason behind the replacement? If you dropped the rep, why? If the rep dropped your line, why?

- *What are some lines that are compatible with yours?* What are some of the competitive lines?

- *What is the commission structure you are paying?* What is your commission payment policy?

- *Will the rep have exclusive sales rights in that territory?*

Under some circumstances it is not really feasible to expect to hire sales reps. Ford says, "If the product sells to galleries it is not appropriate for a rep. If the primary focus is on gallery sales, it is not, in my opinion, a rep-able, line because reps work on volume."

"If they say, 'We're new and we're not selling to anybody,' we generally don't like to take on the line. We suggest that the manufacturer go out and test-market this product first before they pay us for a rep," Ford explains.

Test marketing is important in answering questions like whether their price point is right or if the product has sell-through.

Adds Ford, "They need to know that information first, because a rep won't take on a line unless the manufacturer can say to them with some relative confidence that we have sold this store or these kinds of stores...." These stores tend to be boutiques, Hallmark stores, or gourmet shops.

Ford says that once that question has been answered, "Then the sales rep has a clue as far as where that product belongs. Reps sell in volume and the product must have some sell-through in order to pique their interest to take on a line. They don't want to invest their time and energy in a line for which there is no sell-through, because it's not the initial order, it's the re-order that the rep makes money on. The manufacturers have to know that. So if they haven't test-marketed their product, what they expect of us is unrealistic.

"Once we get the registration form, we prescreen referrals for (sellers), sending them the information that they need on reps," Ford says. "We send them a two-page summary giving them all the information about each of the particular reps that have been prescreened to their product category. We tell them they may get a wonderful response. They may get no response. The discussion is between the manufacturer and the rep directly." If a rep that has been referred by the Rep Registry is hired, then the charge is $140.

"We send a summary sheet with the packet of information on each of the reps. Accompanying the rep profiles are summary sheets with an outcome column where we ask them to tell us what they've heard from the rep. They mail that back, and that's the information needed to rework the account. Manufacturers generally stay on the registry 'forever.'

"The bottom line is, I really have a passion for what I am doin," Ford says, "and I happen to love hand-crafted American products."

SPECIAL FEATURES: "There's a need among very intelligent people who don't know what they're getting into, and unless they educate themselves first, the chances are they will make some mistakes that are avoidable," Ford says. "We put a handbook together to answer the very simple kindergarten-level questions." *Working with Wholesale Giftware Reps...A Beginner's Handbook* offers all types of valuable advice—telling readers what to look out for in contracts, how to interview sales reps, and what to do if the rep hired is not selling.

HOW TO CONTACT: **Rep Registry**
P.O. Box 2306
Capistrano Beach, California 92624

QUESTIONS TO ASK: Can you send me a brochure that explains your services?
How many craftspeople with products like mine find reps through the registry?

CHAPTER **11**

Arts Group Electronic Network

It's New!
Selling
Through an
Arts Group
Electronic
Network

PRODUCTS BUYERS WANT: information for all artists and crafters

COSTS TO CONSIDER: Start-up fee, monthly maintenance charge, and telephone time. Figure on $25 and up. To participate on-line, a computer with a modem is necessary.

The personal computer has emerged as more than just another business tool. Computers have become a communication link just as vital as the telephone or facsimile machine. News and information is available twenty-four hours a day, seven days a week. Information from these convenient on-line services might soon eclipse the news in local newspapers, beating them both in speed of delivery and depth of coverage.

A service called Arts Wire links visual and performing arts groups across the nation and is available as a project of the New York Foundation for the Arts. Arts Wire is a speedy communication and information exchange that effectively addresses several common issues facing artisans and provides new strategies to help artists survive in today's competitive environment. Anne Focke, Arts Wire project coordinator, describes this service as a "computer-based communication network which provides immediate access to news, facts, data, and dialogue on the social, economic, philosophical, intellectual, and political conditions affecting the arts and artists today. Accessing local, regional, and national information about every aspect of the arts from shows to safety through personal computer connected via a modem to your existing phone line benefits all types of artisans."

Some of Arts Wire's organizational partners include the American Craft Council, the Crafts Report, the Center for Safety in the Arts, the Association of Hispanic Arts, American Music Center, Grantmakers in the Arts, National Association of Artists' Organizations, National Campaign for Freedom of Expression, and the National Performance Network. New participants will be welcomed.

The updated information provided through Arts Wire enables artisans not only the opportunity to network but to discover information about upcoming sales opportunities.

SPECIAL FEATURES: Computer information services can be targeted to special audiences and serve as a powerful networking tool among special interest groups. User guides are provided to members.

HOW TO CONTACT: If you have news to give out to Arts Wire's customers or questions about the network, contact:

Arts Wire Front Desk Coordinator
824 South Mill Avenue
Suite 93
Tempe, Arizona 85281
(602) 829-0815. (EMAIL address: ARTSWIRE@TMN.COM)

QUESTIONS TO ASK: What type of information is furnished?
What is the charge for on-line time?
Could you send me a registration packet?

CHAPTER 12

Art in Embassies Program

Display Your Work in Prestigious Locations All over the World

PRODUCTS BUYERS WANT: fine arts and fine crafts

COSTS TO CONSIDER: Submission of slides/transparencies/photographs or examples of artwork may be offered for consideration. Figure on spending $25 or more.

"Embassies represent a unique way for artists to become known in foreign countries," says contemporary artist Frank Stella, a major figure on the American art scene for several decades (from *Art in Embassies: Twenty-Five Years at the U.S. Department of State*). Participation in this prestigious program confers an unequaled distinction, since the honor of being invited to participate in this program can lead to sales and acceptance in other markets not previously open to the artist.

There are 133 embassies in 116 different countries displaying works of art from the Art in Embassies Program (AIEP) valued at more than $40 million. AIEP officials match artwork to the ambassadors' requests from submitted slides. Although the AIEP normally solicits artists through galleries, magazines, and art fairs, they are glad to review unsolicited submissions.

A need for sensitivity to local customs became eminently clear when an abstract painting that bore a date as its title nearly caused a riot in one country.

As it turned out, the date was sacred to the local people, who thought the artist was insulting them. So AIEP carefully developed the following criteria for works to be displayed in American embassies: artwork must be original and created by an American artist; art must be of recognized quality to best represent American culture; and art must be compatible with the cultural concepts and trends of the host country.

SPECIAL FEATURES: AIEP must carefully consider the customs of the host country and the environment where the art would be placed, and must consult with the ambassador and the ambassador's spouse to determine the kind of art they want to display. Additionally, they must consider condition, fragility, suitability for shipping, and exhibition constraints, as well as lender's special requirements.

HOW TO CONTACT: Once received, officials match the artwork to requests, then send the slides to the ambassador for perusal. Next, the selected artwork is placed on temporary loan to their residences. Artists interested in participating in the AIEP should send slides, transparencies, or photographs to:

Art in Embassies Program
U.S. Department of State
Room B258
Washington, D.C. 20520
(202) 647-5723

QUESTIONS TO ASK: How long before I hear if my artwork has been placed?
Can you send me literature about the Art in Embassies Program?

13

Co-op America

PRODUCTS BUYERS WANT: arts and crafts items made by artists and craftspeople with a commitment to society and the environment

---

COSTS TO CONSIDER: long-distance telephone calls and Co-op America membership: individual members, $20 a year; business members, $60 a year

---

Only for Artisans Who Want to Help Our Planet

"Co-op America is more than a catalog selling things. We deeply believe that the thought behind a gift—or any purchase—should include the company that makes it," said Denise Hamler, *Co-op America Catalog* director. "By carefully selecting our purchases, we can send a message to businesses and corporations: respecting and protecting the earth and the people on it are part of a successful equation for running a profitable business."

All products offered in the catalog are guaranteed to come from groups that are socially and environmentally responsible. Hamler defines socially responsible businesses as those that "balance the concerns of all the stakeholders when they make business decisions—consumers, employees, community and the planet." A spirit of cooperation in the workplace must also be practiced. Statistics prove that this catalog company has found its niche. The *Co-op America Catalog* reaches about five hundred thousand people a year, processing about twenty thousand orders. These consumers realize that by purchasing from Co-op America, they can take part in creating a sustainable society and a healthy earth.

Products are chosen for the *Co-op America Catalog* based on whether they meet the most social and environmental criteria. Some closely examined criteria are:

- high quality, well made, and long lasting
- made from renewable or recycled products
- re-usable or recyclable by the consumer
- nontoxic and made from natural materials
- fair price to the consumer
- fair price to the people producing it
- made in a safe, cooperative, and responsible workplace
- supportive of education
- portion of the profit proceeds donated to nonprofit groups
- uses minimal packaging
- promotes life-affirming values
- respectful of all people in all walks of life

Vincente and Rose Gonzales
Woven Mug Rugs
Photo: Co-op America

Co-op America generates several publications in addition to the *Co-op America Catalog*. Its Green Business Program starts and supports small socially and environmentally responsible businesses, the Consumer Education and Empowerment Program tells people how to vote with their dollars to effect change, and the Sustainable Living Program provides information about practical measures people can take to make their personal, community, and work lives more meaningful.

In 1982, the founders of Co-op America reasoned that every time someone makes a purchase, the money spent goes to work. They help direct that purchasing power toward supporting businesses that create jobs, care about their communities, and protect our environment. Co-op America helps consumers locate those businesses and then provides technical assistance to help businesses succeed.

SPECIAL FEATURES: Co-op America membership benefits:

- Free copy of the National Green Pages™.
- Free listing in the National Green Pages™.
- Free subscription to the members-only newsletter, *Co-op America Connections.*
- Free subscription to *The Co-op America Quarterly.*
- Free subscription to *Boycott Action News.*
- Free access to credit card processing services at competitive rates, through a bank committed to social and environmental investing.
- Free consultation on socially responsible investing and employee retirement plans.

HOW TO CONTACT:

Artists or crafters can contact (publications also available from):

Co-op America Business Network

1850 M Street, N.W., Suite 700

P.O. Box 18217

Washington, D.C. 20036

(202) 872-5307, or fax (202) 331-8166

QUESTIONS TO ASK:

Can you send me the *Co-op America Catalog*?

Do you have any literature about the selection criteria?

AVAILABLE PUBLICATIONS:

The Co-op America Catalog (free)

Mail-order collection of products from only socially and environmentally responsible businesses.

Co-op America's National Green Pages ($4.95, free to members)

The largest directory of America's leading socially and environmentally responsible businesses.

Co-op America Quarterly ($20 a year, free to members)

Information on how consumer power can improve the environment.

The Hummer Family
Cedar Heart
Photo: Co-op America

Co-op America Catalog

A tasty treat from the Betty Clooney Foundation located in Long Beach, California, is promoted in the *Co-op America Catalog* as, "Give a breakfast that gives twice." Listed as such because each woven basket—filled with buttermilk pancake mix, wildflower honey complete with dipper, and raspberry syrup—that is ordered raises money for support programs for survivors of brain damage. Picking, packaging, and selling their fresh produce gives young adults who have sustained brain injuries the opportunity to learn new memory patterns, regain motor skills, and slowly rebuild their self-esteem.

Bold, splashy prints with wild patterns inspired by street murals hand-screened on shower curtains will liven up anyone's morning routine. Each curtain that is hung in a home helps create jobs for talented young Harlem artists. These all-cotton shower curtains were designed by artistic students from the Children's Art Carnival, then printed at the Harlem Textile Works. It is the only black independent textile design and production firm operating in Harlem. This collaborative process brings desperately needed jobs in design, printing, color mixing, screen making, and stitching into the area. The funds raised go to the Children's Art Carnival which provides art and craft classes in subjects ranging from collage to creative writing.

Colleen's Garden, a native-owned family business in South Dakota, produces crafts during the long winter. The company's Sioux Scent is blended with a

Chet and Colleen Cordell
Hand-thrown Ceramic Cache Jar
Photo: Co-op America

prairie plant that legend says, "encourages healing spirits," and comes packed in a hand-thrown ceramic cache jar.

All of these products are offered through Co-op America, a nonprofit institution committed to supporting businesses that demonstrate caring and respect for their customers, employees, community, and the earth. The founders believe that their job is to link these businesses to people who value peace, justice, cooperation and a healthy planet, saying, "It's easy to get involved in the movement for peace, cooperation, and a healthy planet—you do it every day with your spending and savings—money! Co-op America believes that the money you spend and save gives you power to direct it away from destructive, inhumane activities and toward those that are healthy, cooperative, and peaceful. That's why we started this catalog. We search out the best: products that inspire and affirm life from businesses that play a role in building a just and sustainable society. By purchasing the socially responsible and environmentally sound alternatives in our catalog, you, in turn, show that values like peace, cooperation, and ecology have a place in our economy."

Another Native American firm represented inside the pages of the *Co-op America Catalog* is Ute Mountain Indian Pottery, whose plant is wholly tribal-owned. Over twenty artists are employed to cast the pottery, then hand-paint, glaze, and fire Ute Mountain mugs. According to the catalog, "These artists' original designs are drawn from the contours of the mountains, canyons and mesas, and from the colors of the desert under the sun, clouds, and stars." These contemporary re-creations reinterpret distinctive Ute motifs. "The making of highly decorated pottery was perfected by the Utes and their ancestors the Anasazi over seven centuries ago." By discovering its heritage, this tribe might find the key to its continued existence.

Respect for the surrounding community takes another turn in Asheville, North Carolina. When many workers were left unemployed after large textile mills—owned by outsiders—moved overseas in search of lower wages, High Cotton made a commitment not only to the former textile workers but to the visually impaired. Now the business produces heavy-duty cotton duckcloth toiletry bags. Co-op America also encourages environmental responsibility. Skyflight Mobiles, whose craftsmen bring silk-screened birds of the wilderness such as the Eagle, Heron, Loon, Mallard, and Canada Goose into homes, donates a portion of its profits to conservation groups. Dream Feather Productions introduces contemporary designs by Yaqui artist Stan Padilla. "The all-cotton shirts are produced entirely by Native Americans, with a portion of the proceeds supporting the continuation of Indian ceremonies and the education of native American youths."

A myriad of small businesses are also well represented in the *Co-op America Catalog*. The Hummers of Texas hand carve intricate boxes with heart drawers from dead cedar that has either fallen or been left over from the fence post industry, never cutting live trees. Hand-rolled, long-burning beeswax candles are handmade at Cat Holler Candles, a woman-owned business in Olive Hill, Tennessee, and "Seasong" wind chimes from Openayre soothe the ears with sounds made by polished aluminum rods hung from Oregon-coast driftwood.

Handmade wool coasters that keep surfaces safe from wet glasses are crafted by New Mexico artisans Rose and Vicente Gonzales and their three children. The chile design is actually woven into the wool utilizing traditional hand carving, dyeing, spinning, and weaving skills. These gifted artisans want to help another generation learn to use their creativity to earn a living.

Harlem Textile Works
Hand-screened Cotton Cap
Photo: Co-op America

What started as a sixteen-page insert in a small magazine in 1981 has grown to a forty-eight-page, twice-yearly publication that reaches five hundred thousand people annually, doing $1 million a year in business. Co-op America features more than three hundred products from 105 socially and environmentally responsible businesses ranging from cooperatives, worker-owned companies, "green" businesses, nonprofit corporations, community self-help groups, family-owned farms, minority/women-owned businesses, and companies employing and empowering the disadvantaged.

Co-op America's best-selling T-shirt seems to summarize the founders' philosophy. This bright yellow T-shirt designed by the Women's International League for Peace and Freedom states simply, "It will be a great day when our schools get all the money they need and the Air Force has to hold a bake sale to buy a bomber."

Lynne Rutherford
"Your Bag of Tricks"
(Handpainted Fabric Dye
on Muslin)
See related information in
Chapter 17
Photo: Lynne Rutherford

The Textile Detective

WANTED:	textile artists who want to sell their teaching skills
COSTS TO CONSIDER:	Registration fee: $30 (listing/four issues). Includes free copy of *The Textile Detective's Guidelines for Teachers Giving Lectures and Workshops.*

Florence Feldman-Wood loves nothing more than solving a good mystery. As an accomplished spinner/weaver, she believed that many textile artists would like to share their extensive knowledge with others. To help them do this, she created The Textile Detective, an information registry for speakers and teachers in basketry, knitting, quilting, surface design, weaving/spinning, and dyeing.

The Teacher Directory is available to guilds and craft groups in the United States and Canada who want to acquire the services of an instructor to hold workshops for artisans or speakers to address groups. Created as an information service rather than a booking agency, The Textile Detective leaves fee information and formal arrangements up to the teachers and show or guild organizers. The directories, containing the names of teachers of fiber or fabric crafts, are updated quarterly since new members are constantly being added. *The Teacher Directory* lists participants by their craft category providing names, addresses, and travel preferences, along with a brief summary of the lectures and workshops which are offered. The Textile Detective wants to take the mystery out of acquiring teaching talent. Their services are advertised in major textile magazines, as well as sending direct mailings to numerous craft organizations.

SPECIAL FEATURE: If an artist wants to teach basketry, knitting, quilting, surface design, weaving/spinning, and dyeing, or find a qualified instructor in any of these areas, then The Textile Detective may be able to solve his or her problem.

HOW TO CONTACT:

For clues about *The Teacher Directory*, contact:

The Textile Detective
P.O. Box 422
Andover, Massachusetts 01810
(508) 475-8790

QUESTIONS TO ASK:

How much is the annual renewal fee?
Do you have any literature about your organization to send me?

CHAPTER 15

ArtNetwork

PRODUCTS BUYERS WANT:	visual arts (computer fine art, mixed media, neon art, painting, photography, sculpture and watercolor)
COSTS TO CONSIDER:	*Artworld Hotline Newsletter*—twenty-four issues (one year), $26, twelve issues (six months), $16 *Art Marketing Sourcebook*—$21.95 *ArtSource Quarterly*—eight issues (two years), $34, four issues (one year), $19, current issue, $6
MAILING LISTS:	500 foreign galleries—$55 560 art museums—$70 640 interior designers—$55

Visual artists can now easily find facts on funding, galleries, commissions, scholarships, and consultants by looking for artists and jobs in the arts via information from a newsletter by ArtNetwork in Renaissance, California. In a recent *Artworld Hotline Newsletter*, a consulting firm for interior designers in the hospitality, corporate, and high-end residential field searched for new artists for major hotel installations. In that same issue, the City of Carlsbad asked California artists to apply for possible inclusion on the design team for Alta Mira Community Park.

ArtNetwork also publishes *Art Marketing Sourcebook*, a guide to art galleries, curators, museums, sales representatives, and dealers that can directly lead to sales for artwork. Information is kept current on a yearly basis.

ArtNetwork offers customized mailing lists along with general lists of categories such as foreign galleries, art museums, and interior designers, if targeting a specific market is desirable. Examples include New York City galleries, Texas art reps and corporations, and Chicago art organizations.

Additionally, ArtNetwork publishes *ArtSource Quarterly*, a good way to keep in contact with art world professionals. Each issue focuses on a specific area: Summer—Art Publishers, Fall—Galleries, Winter—Reps/Consultants, and Spring—Art Organizations.

SPECIAL FEATURE: Allows artists opportunities to explore potential markets without having to perform all the necessary research on their own.

HOW TO CONTACT: **ArtNetwork**
P.O. Box 369
13284 Rices Crossing Road
Renaissance, California 95962
(800) 383-0677 or (916) 692-1355, or fax (916) 692-1370

QUESTIONS TO ASK: Could you send free information about your company's information for artists?

BOOK: *Art Marketing Handbook for the Fine Artist*
ArtNetwork, Constance Franklin-Smith
P.O. Box 369
13284 Rices Crossing Road
Renaissance, California 95962

CHAPTER 16

Museums

*Be Invited
to Join
the Elite*

PRODUCTS BUYERS WANT: fine arts and fine crafts

COSTS TO CONSIDER: Long-distance telephone calls, slides, and shipping. Figure on about $25 or more.

Every artist dreams of exhibiting work in a prestigious museum. Standard ways to achieve this goal are to be invited by one of the eighty-two hundred museums located in America to take part in an exhibition, to be selected for a juried exhibition, or to sell or donate work to a museum. It is important to realize that these institutions are regularly opening more doors to new artists. Artists must carefully outline their own approach as far as making inquiries to museums. Usually, the first action that leads to museum exhibitions is preparation of a set of slides, a resumé, and a show proposal.

Step 1—Slides

Museums are often willing to look at artists' slides, which are sometimes referred to as transparencies. Even the Guggenheim Museum has a "viewing program." Most of the time, curators at the more prestigious museums in New York and elsewhere prefer slides be sent by mail, while others voice no objection to a personal visit. Anyone with an interest in exhibiting should first contact the museum by telephone to ascertain its procedure for submissions. Directors normally prefer that slides be sent by mail. However, after a personal telephone conversation, they may agree to a meeting.

Step 2—Resumés

A resumé should be included along with the slides. The specific purpose of an artist's resumé is to impress curators. This resumé must persuade the interviewer that the artist has achieved prominence in the arts field. Subjects such as education, group exhibitions, solo shows, commissions, awards, and honors are listed. Care should be taken to build these essential credentials. Sometimes artists enter national competitive shows described in magazines such as *American Artist* to begin building their reputation. Often universities and museums sponsor contests. These institutions can be contacted directly for information about upcoming events.

Finally, adding a bibliography gives artists the chance to add significant details from their career. Photographs, especially those that portray the artist at work, often help establish credibility.

Step 3—Proposals

The artist's proposal should describe his or her idea, purpose, motivation, and intended audience for the work. This write-up should tell why the selected theme is significant, how the subject will be developed, and who will be involved in all stages of the implementation. Space or site requirements need to be carefully designated. All of the exhibition factors—advance planning, preparation, presentation, packing, illumination, and installation—also must be considered and handled.

After the slides, resumé, and proposal have been prepared, the artist should check to see if there are any museums that might be interested in the work and whether or not those museums hold viewing days. If so, an appointment to present his or her best artwork should be made as soon as materials can be properly prepared. It is important for the artist to arrive for the viewing on time or early. By doing so, respect is shown for the person(s) willing to make the time to interview aspiring artists. Curators know how to allow enough time to see artistic work. Be careful to limit the presentation to the stated time unless the interviewer extends an invitation to continue further.

Museum curators must continuously organize exhibitions, assemble collections, and oversee the production of catalogs. Often they are under pressure to discover new movements and to promote theme-based exhibitions. Curators know that at times they must search beyond the well-known artists if they want to accomplish the museum's long-range goals. Curators continue on a constant quest to discover artists with a distinctive artistic point of view. The following approaches can help aspiring artists gain an audience with curators:

- *Determine the viewing policies of the museum.* With one telephone call, the artist can determine the institution's policies concerning new submissions.

- *Visit the museum regularly throughout the year.* Read all of the museum's catalogs in order to get a sense of taste and direction. These visits will also be helpful in determining the director's and curator's interests.

- *A museum is seldom the place for a first exhibition.* Try to gain visibility at commercial galleries, schools, banks, and alternative spaces first.

- *If represented by a gallery, encourage the gallery owner to show the work to various museums.*

Once an artist's work has been accepted by a museum, he or she should begin thinking about the legal and financial details involved. Arrangements made with museums demand written agreements. As soon as a showing situation arises, it is important to lay the groundwork to prevent future misunderstandings. Immediately put the agreement in writing. An artist should respect his/her work enough not only to hold out for the best possible deal, but to get all commitments in writing.

If an artist is invited to exhibit at a museum, a curator will probably present a contract. Most museums offer standard contracts detailing the terms concerning the loan of a work for an exhibition. It is important to remember that each term may be subject to negotiation. If a contract is not presented, ask for one. Generally museum loan agreements cover the following:

1. *Loss or damage.* This designates exactly who is responsible for the work and at what times.

2. *Evaluation of value.* Determination of how much the artwork is worth.

3. *Insurance coverage.* Exactly who is responsible for providing insurance and at what times.

4. *Option to buy.* Determine whether or not the museum has an interest in purchasing.

5. *Restoration and repair.* Specify who will supervise and pay for damages.

6. *Framing.* The museum is probably not going to pay additional framing costs, even when an artist has been invited to exhibit. Be prepared for this added expense.

One way for artists to gain entry into museums is by entering regional and local juried exhibitions. Often these exhibitions are juried by notable museum officials from all over the country. Many artists have been discovered through juried exhibitions. Following is a partial listing of museum competitions:

Contemporary Artifacts Show
National Museum of American Jewish History
55 North Fifth Street
Philadelphia, Pennsylvania 19106
(215) 923-3811

National Ceramic Competition
San Angelo Museum of Fine Arts
Box 3092
San Angelo, Texas 76902
(915) 658-4084

Northwest International Arts Competition

Whatcom Museum of History and Art
121 Prospect Street
Bellingham, Washington 98225
(206) 676-6981

SPECIAL FEATURES: Participation in either a group or a large juried exhibition can make an incredibly positive impact on an artist's professional life. This is especially true when competition is strong for a juried show or when an artist is asked by a curator to participate in a special by-invitation-only exhibit, which allows the artist to select the pieces to be shown. As always, museum "solo" shows offer the greatest prestige.

Artists or crafters of fine art objects can find lists of museums through the following:

HOW TO CONTACT:

Compuname

411 Theodore Fremd Avenue
Rye, New York 10580-1497
Provides labels with names and addresses of all entries in the *Art in America Guide to Galleries, Museums, and Artists*, including museums, galleries, private dealers, art consultants, university galleries, and publishers.

Caroll Michels

491 Broadway
New York, New York 10012
Offers various arts-related mailing lists that include the names and addresses of curators, art consultants, critics and press. Updated several times a year.

HOW TO CONTACT: Artists or crafters can find museums through the following publications:

American Art Directory 1993-94

> R.R. Bowker
> 121 Chanlon Road
> New Providence, New Jersey 07974
> A directory of arts organizations, art schools, museums, magazines, scholarships, and fellowships published triennially.

Directory of Artist Associations and Exhibition Spaces, Art Commissions, Museum Curators, and Art Critics

> Directors Guild Publishers and The Consultant Press
> P.O. Box 369
> 13284 Rices Crossing Road
> Renaissance, California 95962

International Directory of the Arts

> Wittenborn Art Books, Inc.
> 1018 Madison Avenue
> New York, New York 10021-0163
> Two-volume guide to museums, universities, associations, dealers, galleries, publishers, and others involved in the arts in Europe, the United States, Canada, South America, Asia, and Australia revised biannually.

The Official Museum Directory

> R.R. Bowker
> 121 Chanlon Road
> New Providence, New Jersey 07974
> Lists more than sixty-six hundred museums and galleries, and includes information on personnel, collections, and specialization.

Art Marketing Sourcebook for the Fine Artist
ArtNetwork
P.O. Box 369
13284 Rices Crossing Road
Renaissance, California 95962
(800) 383-0677, or fax (916) 692-1370
Listing of museums throughout the United States that indicates if they are making purchases.

QUESTIONS TO ASK:

Will the museum insure exhibited works?
Who decides the monetary value of my work for insurance purposes?
Will a museum charge a commission if a work is sold?
If I donate a work of art, can I request a permanent display?
If I sell my work, will the museum want the copyright?
Will I get royalties for reproductions?

FOR INFORMATION ON SLIDES, RESUMÉS, AND PROPOSALS:

Slides:

Handbook for Contemporary Photography, Arnold Gassan, Rochester, New York: Light Impressions
Basic Photography, M.J. Langford, Stoneham, Massachusetts: Focal Press
Craft of Photography, David Vestal, New York: Harper and Row
Photography for the Art Market, Kathryn Marx, New York: Watson-Guptill
Photographing Your Artwork, Russell Hart, Cincinnati, Ohio: Northlight Books

Resumés:

The Resumé Writer's Handbook, Michael Holley Smith, New York: Harper and Row
Resumés That Work: How to Sell Yourself on Paper, Loretta D. Foxman, edited by Walter L. Polsky, New York: Wiley
Resumé Writing: A Comprehensive How-to-Do-It Guide, edited by Burdette E. Bostwick, New York: Wiley

Resumé Handbook: How to Write Outstanding Resumés and Cover Letters, Bob Adamas, Holbrook, Massachusetts

Resumé Software:

PFS: Resumé and Job Search Professional (Spinnaker)

Proposal Writing:

The Art of Showing, James K. Reeve, Smithsonian Institution Traveling Exhibition Service, Washington, D.C. 20506

Getting Funded: A Complete Guide to Proposal Writing, Mary Stewart Hall, Continuing Education Publications, Portland State University, P.O. Box 1491, Portland, Oregon 97207

The Proposal Writer's Guide, Michael Burns, Development and Technical Assistance Center, 70 Audubon Street, New Haven, Connecticut 06510, (203) 772-1345.

Private Showings

PRODUCTS BUYERS WANT: arts and crafts

COSTS TO CONSIDER: Invitations (and/or promotional materials), packaging materials, and refreshments. Estimated cost: $50 and up.

Private showings help artists sell all types of work. A private art showing is like an elegant craft fair. Enticing invitations accompanied by brochures are sent to carefully selected prospects, followed by a friendly personal phone call a week or so later.

Artisan Lynne Rutherford's "Trunk Shows" feature her concept of "Come and Go!" which means that attendees are invited to arrive any time during the hours of the show. Rutherford encourages guests to bring as many friends as they wish. She estimates that out of every one hundred invitations sent, normally thirty to fifty attend.

Rutherford's Fall Trunk Shows highlight jewelry accessories specially designed for the season that celebrates football, turkey, and evergreen. Invitees can browse through racks of blouses, shirts, skirts, jackets, and vests, and examine jewelry in display cases strategically placed in every corner of each room.

A private showing should emphasize customer service by providing helpful information about the specifics involved with the art or craft work. Perhaps a color consultant could be invited to assist customers in selecting shades that highlight their skin tone and hair color. If artwork is suitable for home decor, then interior designers could be invited to give attendees professional advice.

Rutherford says, "The best months for my parties are in the winter from mid-October to mid-December and in the spring—March and April. Summer sales have never been that good, so I use that time to create new designs for the next year."

Some of Rutherford's parties are reciprocal-type events. For instance, there has been a Fall Trunk Show hosted by a Mary Kay consultant. People benefit by exchanging information about customers. For agreeing to give a party, the hostess receives 10 percent of the total sales for the day in free Vintage Modern merchandise. Rutherford's sales materials are bright and colorful:

Lynne Rutherford
Charm Necklace with Earrings
Photo: Lynne Rutherford

Invitations
The invitations are printed on orange stock that is postcard-size. They encourage invitees to do their holiday shopping early! When and where the event is being held is listed, along with Rutherford's address and telephone number.

Information Sheets
If anyone shows interest in hosting a party in the future, Rutherford supplies a sunshine-yellow information sheet stating, "If You Would Like To Host A Vintage Modern Party, There Are Some Guidelines" and gives a description of "Vintage Modern Home Parties."

Tags
Each piece of jewelry is attached to a (Vintage Modern) card which includes a logo along with a line at the bottom saying, "Designed and hand-crafted by Lynne Rutherford." Every clothing item has a tag stating, "Each piece is an original design, hand-painted by the artist just for you," along with the size and price.

Packaging

All purchases should be packaged then packed with great care, possibly in seasonally decorated gift boxes. Classy velvet pads and beveled-glass mirrors could be provided to aid customers viewing merchandise. In addition, the hostess might ask those invited to wear solid-colored, dressy clothing, which makes a magnificent background for hand-crafted wearables and jewelry.

Hostess Guidelines for Lynne Rutherford's Vintage Modern Parties

■ *Scheduling the Party.* All parties should be arranged at least one month in advance. This amount of time allows for invitations to be properly prepared and promptly mailed. Rutherford provides both the invitations and the stamps. All the hostess has to do is the addressing and see that they are mailed.

■ *Party Times.* Rutherford's Vintage Modern parties are always "come and go" as guests please. They can last from three to eight hours, depending on the wishes of the host.

■ *Party Setup.* Rutherford needs approximately one-and-a-half hours before the party to set up the merchandise-for-sale-display.

■ *How Many People to Invite.* The more people invited, the more who will come, thus giving the party the greatest chance for success. Usually hosts invite anywhere from fifty to one hundred fifty or more. Invitations can be extended to professional groups, church friends, and any others who might be interested.

■ *What about Refreshments?* Snacks and drinks are supplied by the hostess, and can be whatever she likes. Some provide cookies; others serve hors d'oeuvres.

■ *Hostess Percentage.* The hostess receives 10 percent of the total sales for the day, in free Vintage Modern merchandise. Gifts may be selected from items in stock or by custom order.

SPECIAL FEATURES: These private showings furnish the ideal opportunity for artisans to try out new styles to see how well their works will sell. The intimacy involved with customers in a private setting provides direct consumer feedback which can determine whether new pieces should be added to lines for the next season. Showings also provide a way to sell leftover samples and close-out items.

HOW TO CONTACT: Start by making a list of people who like artistic items. Include all organizations, clubs, and groups located in the area that might express interest in an elegant presentation of artisan's work.

QUESTIONS TO ASK: What is the policy in regard to returns?
What happens if items are accidentally broken?
What about refreshments for guests?
How is the host or hostess compensated?

BOOKS *Home Boutiques—A Profitable Alternative to Selling at Craft Fairs*
by Lynn Ocken
3518 Heatheridge Drive
Cedar Rapids, Iowa 52402
Provides information gathered through personal experience

A Guide to Marketing Crafts Through a Home Party System
by JoMucha and Marion Boyer
Village Vendor, Ltd.
8500 Valleywood Lane
Kalamazoo, Michigan 49002
Step-by-step guidelines for putting on home shows

CHAPTER 18

Procurement Automated Source System (PASS)

Put Your Taxes to Work— for You!

PRODUCTS BUYERS WANT: products made by U.S. citizens

COSTS TO CONSIDER: free

"Take advantage of a great opportunity to sell your products to the federal government and its prime contractors." This is the message given in literature put out by U.S. Small Business Administration (SBA). The SBA has a program that puts a company's name right in front of hundreds of government purchasing agents at no cost to the participating business!

All that is required is to fill out a simple form. Once the SBA receives the completed form, this general information is listed in an on-line computerized directory of small businesses called the Procurement Automated Source System (PASS). This information is basically what owners usually tell potential clients about their work.

Each day PASS is not only used by large defense contractors such as Boeing and Lockheed, but also by numerous federal agencies, including the departments of defense, commerce, agriculture, and energy. These federal agencies and their contractors are required to buy from small businesses. Their purchasing agents have found PASS to be a fast and effective tool to find sources of products. PASS is also searched to identify minority and small firms for possible subcontracting opportunities. Many small businesses have experienced great success as a result of their products being listed on this computerized system. Keep in mind that in 1993, the government spent $180 billion on goods and services.

SPECIAL FEATURE: A listing in the Procurement Automated Source System is free! The government even pays the postage for the form to be mailed.

HOW TO CONTACT: Look up regional or district U.S. Small Business Administration offices in the "blue pages" section of the business pages in the telephone book, or call your local or regional U.S. Small Business Administration, or (800) U-ASK-SBA.

QUESTIONS TO ASK: Could you send me the SBA/PASS form?
How long will it take for my business to be registered once I return my form to SBA?

CHAPTER 19

Boston Corporate Art

PRODUCTS BUYERS WANT: fine art

COSTS TO CONSIDER: Slides will cost about $25. If work is accepted, expect to pay negotiated fees.

Knowing the Right People to Call

Boston Corporate Art, an advisory and consulting firm, has helped artists secure important corporate connections since 1986. So even if an artist is located hundreds of miles from a metropolitan area, he or she can still successfully sell their work to major corporate clients. John Kirby, president of Boston Corporate Art, states, "We have well over one thousand artists in our slide files that we regularly access." All of their artists are located or represented within the contiguous United States.

Kirby goes on to explain that Boston Corporate Art retains a permanent slide registry of artists' work in virtually all media. "We handle all different types of art from limited edition posters to sculpture, tapestry, and oils on canvas." Each submission is considered on a periodic year-round basis for corporate presentations. Occasionally, Boston Corporate Art will request fine artwork on approval if client interest is high and the potential for placement appears possible. If for some reason art must be returned to the artist, Boston Corporate Art normally accepts responsibility for return crating, shipping, and the necessary insurance.

Kirby says that they have "hundreds and hundreds and hundreds" of corporate clients ranging from the enormous IBM to medium-sized firms such as John Hancock to smaller firms such as Grove Bank. In fact, Kirby challenges, "Name a company and we've probably done some work for them." Their function since they began operations in 1986 has been to assist corporations in the acquisition of fine art and to commission site-specific work by interfacing with the corporate community.

Selected artists are asked to send slides to corporate clients such as insurance companies, restaurants, hospitals, and nursing-home communities for review. Although most client attention comes from the immediate Boston area, many times these corporations buy for their subsidiaries located in other states.

SPECIAL FEATURE: Boston Corporate Art provides a method of reaching corporations, insurance companies, restaurants, and health-care communities that would neither be accessible nor affordable for most artists to pursue.

HOW TO CONTACT:

Boston Corporate Art
Art Consulting
470 Atlantic Avenue
Boston, Massachusetts 02210
(617) 426-8880, or fax (617) 426-5551

QUESTIONS TO ASK:

What services does your firm provide?
How often is artwork requested on approval?
How many clients do you already have that are in my artistic area?

CHAPTER 20

Trade Publications

PRODUCTS BUYERS WANT: arts and crafts

COSTS TO CONSIDER: cost of subscriptions, ranging anywhere from $24 per year on up

---

There are several good trade publications available for artists and crafters. These magazines provide all types of interesting information. One of the best-known periodicals in the craft community is *The Crafts Report*, often hailed as "the business journal for the crafts industry." Pioneered by Michael Scott, the magazine was started in 1975 as an eight-page, 8½" x 11" newsletter with a main purpose of helping craftspeople find markets for their work. Editor Marilyn Stevens affirms the fact that *The Crafts Report* "has evolved along with the crafts movement. We are really committed to helping craftspeople make a living at the work they love to do. We do that by finding out what they need to know. My staff and our freelancers are always going out to crafts shows, calling craftspeople and asking them, 'What are your issues? What have you come upon?' That's where we get the bulk of our ideas—from actual situations or issues that craftspeople deal with, whether it's in the health-care arena, finding alternate sources for marketing, dealing with their taxes, shipping, traveling, or whatever. We're always trying to keep our antennas out in order to see what's going on."

Often *The Crafts Report* prints articles that can directly help artisans sell their work. For example, they did a story on the Oregon Potters Association (OPA) explaining how small specialty restaurants make good customers for functional pottery. Restaurants have a recurring need for products. They pointed out that restaurant chains offer even greater potential for huge sales.

The Crafts Report quoted from the OPA newsletter, which suggested that pottery for such restaurants needs to be exceptionally tough and chip-resistant since steam tables and sterilizing dishwashers exert more than average stress. Potters were advised that:

- Restaurant dinnerware should be guaranteed against thermal shock.

- Cross sections of one-fourth inch or more, and smooth, easy-to-clean surfaces should be the rule.

- Avoid curlicue designs or jutting lips.

- Potters also must design the pottery to size, using liquid measure so that containers hold a specific number of ounces.

In Nelson, New Zealand, restaurateurs Miranda and Ben van Dyke customized their table service by commissioning thirty local potters to create six original cups and saucers each. Then the van Dykes serve every customer with a different style coffee cup, choosing those designs which best suit different types of customers.

Once readers find out about this as a possible market, they can then go to the library for further research. From reference books, they can learn about the twenty thousand active members of the National Restaurant Association who may be interested in acquiring pottery for their food operations.

For more information, they can write to the National Restaurant Association, 1200 17th Street, N.W., Washington, D.C. 20036, or consult local yellow pages under Restaurants. These types of stories can offer leads that, if followed, can earn crafters more income. In addition to articles, such as the one on pottery, there are several other areas within *The Crafts Report* which should be of interest to small businesses.

Courtney Miller and
Lee Peterson
"Bumble Bee" (Sterling Silver
and Brass Pin/Pendant)
Featured in Crafts Report's
Craft Showcase
*Photo: Crocker Studio, Inc.
Photography*
©1993

Mark Beck, owner of the Craft Center, a craft mall in Vermont, suggests crafters consult "the national bible of the crafters, *The Crafts Report,* for the latest in news that concerns the arts and crafts community. *The Crafts Report* has features on subjects such as trade shows, crafts guilds and business hothouses; news items about late-breaking events; and advice columns about law, photography, and health. The "Departments" section includes announcements on competitions, conferences, and exhibitions. "Crafts Available" offers classified advertising for all types of artistic work from clothing accessories to wood. A special section at the end of each issue, "Crafts Wanted" lists shops and galleries that are actively looking for items to sell. In December 1993, "Craft Showcase," a four-color advertising section premiered, offering what Editor Marilyn Stevens terms, "the best work by the most sought-after craft artisans in the country."

"The Crafts Report has been very good for us as far as (generating) business. They are really a pleasure to work with," says Joei Skesfington, owner of Crafters Showcase in Paramus, New Jersey. She emphasizes that *The Crafts Report* has "great articles, very informative. They are wonderful to work with; their readership is good. When we placed a (December display) ad in there the response was amazing!"

Stevens is adamant about the fact that crafts are vital to our country's economy: "We're also very committed to the idea of educating the general public and especially the movers and shakers in government and business of the whole idea of how important crafts are as economic development." They are constantly working to get crafts thought of as a way of life that is absolutely essential. "I do think that the Clinton Administration with its gathering of crafts, both for their holiday tree and the permanent craft collection, is helping. The Year of the American Craft helped as well."

Courtney Miller and
Lee Peterson
"Bubba Eats Fish" (Sterling Silver
and Brass Pin/Pendant)
Featured in Crafts Report's
Craft Showcase
Photo: Crocker Studio, Inc.
Photography
©1993
Alyssa Levitan

SPECIAL FEATURE: Each innovative issue educates, entertains, and inspires the reader, from readers' letters in the front to the listing of galleries and shops actively looking for artisans' work in the back. Subscription rate: $24 per year for twelve issues; single issue, $3.95 (available in some bookstores). Write to *The Crafts Report*, 300 Water Street, Wilmington, Delaware 19801, (800) 777-7098 or (302) 656-2209.

QUESTIONS TO ASK: Can you send me information about the "Craft Showcase"?
How much does it cost to advertise in the classified section of *The Crafts Report?*
What is the circulation?

CHAPTER 21

Hotel Gift Shops

*Target
Travelers
with
Your Arts
and Crafts*

....

PRODUCTS BUYERS WANT: arts and crafts

....

COSTS TO CONSIDER: Long-distance telephone, samples, mailing, and shipping expenses. Costs start at $25.

....

Many times hotel gift-shop buyers are quite interested in buying local artisans' work in an effort to give the guests a sample of the ambiance of the region. One of the shops in the Loews Anatole Hotel in Dallas, Texas, specializes in giving its international visitors a glimpse of items that tourists like to view as Texan.

"There are western stores in Dallas, for instance, at the West End. They carry a lot of cowboy boots, cowboy hats, some jewelry, and a lot of western clothing, where 'Strictly Western' carries more novelty items," said Kathy Wood, buyer for the Howard Crow Company, which operates all specialty shops in Loews Anatole Hotels. This western shop features photographs of working ranches, hand-painted gauze broomstick skirts, and Indian-crafted jewelry purchased from southwest Indian artists.

In another part of Dallas, the buyer at the Raddison, a large hotel chain, is attracted to souvenir-type items like Dallas Cowboy mugs which serve as reminders to guests of their trip to "Big D." As with these two buyers, each hotel's gift shop tries to compete by selling different types of arts and crafts.

Gift shops need artists and craftspeople who want to work with them. Just consider the fact that most gift shops are part of a chain, so the potential for selling large amounts of arts and crafts work multiply accordingly. Hotel gift shops remain in business by collecting unusual and/or innovative items that tourists love to take back home.

SPECIAL FEATURE: The American Hotel and Motel Association has over eighty-nine hundred members. This association publishes an annual directory called the *American Hotel and American Motel Leadership Directory* available to non-members for $50. It also publishes a *Construction and Modernization Report* monthly.

....

HOW TO CONTACT: **The American Hotel and Motel Association**
1201 New York Avenue N.W.
Suite 600
Washington, D.C. 20005
(202) 289-3100

....

QUESTIONS TO ASK: Do you allow displays to be set up at your conventions?
Will you take arts and crafts items on consignment?
Would you prefer a brochure or a sample of my work?

Buyer for the Loews
Anatole Hotel Gift Shops

O ne of the most extensive collections of art and antiquities ever assembled outside a museum is housed in the Loews Anatole in Dallas, Texas, the largest hotel in America's Southwest. The double-atrium, high-rise structure contains items as diverse as a pair of Ming Dynasty stone lions and a landscape tapestry woven with four hundred pounds of wool by self-taught Fort Worth weaver Winston Herbert. Beneath a splendid stained-glass skylight, an attractive shopping promenade features the handiwork of various American artisans priced from $2 to ten thousand dollars, showcased in five gift shops.

Kathy Wood, buyer for the Howard Crow Company, the corporation responsible for operation of all specialty shops located in the Loews Anatole Hotel, urges artisans to "do their homework and go to a store first and see what kind of merchandise they carry before they make a phone call or send a sample." The first question she usually asks is, "Have you ever been in the stores before?" If an artisan has, then he or she will know why his/her item might be suitable, what the competition is, and if his/her prices are on target.

The Potpourri features hand-thrown ceramic originals in the display windows, no two pieces alike, from Louisiana artist Jane Adams. At the yearly Dallas Artfest, Wood discovered a Colorado artisan who handcrafts pitchers, plates, and tiles. A Dallas artist, found at Canalfest, held annually at Las Colinas, creates a ceramic chip and dip server which became a best seller even though it retails for more than $50. A New Mexico artist, who, according to Wood, is "flexible and easy to work with," hand paints delicate roses on various types of pottery. An Oklahoma artist designs special trivets, coasters, and trays for the shop.

The Children's Shop carries teddy bears and pillows made with antique quilts from Fredericksburg, Texas. Children's embroidered towel wrap-ups, hand-decorated T-shirts, and sequined sneakers come from Phoenix, Arizona. The walls are lined with colorful prints of clowns made by a Dallas artist and well-suited for any kid's room. Freestanding wood pulp paper dolls known as "Crayon Kids" are hand-crafted by an Arkansas artisan. The minute Wood saw the paper dolls displayed at the Dallas Market Center, she perceived them as tailor-made for The Children's Shop. "I think they (artisans) need to look for voids in the markets and really fill those." There is no overt competition for the Crayon Kids paper dolls because the price is right, the quality is good, the guests love them, and best of all—there is nothing else like them in the marketplace.

The Four Corners Shop boasts items from countries around the world such as Austria, England, France, Poland, and Russia. American artisans contribute arrangements of dried roses, elaborate silver picture frames and pewter replicas of antique-design luggage tags.

Wood clarifies, saying, "Work needs to look professionally done." While some artists selling to the Loews Anatole Hotel gift shops work from their homes, their items are always professionally finished, perfectly acceptable merchandise for a retail setting.

The Collage features mugs hand crafted by Anna Horton Hobbs alongside Texas black-and-white painted cow pottery mugs and dishes. The shop carries delicious food items like hot sauces and chili con queso, provided that the packaging looks "as good as the food." For instance, the jalapeño jelly comes in a jar with a distinct southwest label and a top with a gingham-checked lid encircled by a ribbon with a colorful blue bow.

"Doing craft fairs before talking with retailers is good because (artists) can get an introduction to the public and really see what sells best," Kathy Wood explains, "because the same customer who goes to the crafts fair really is going to be shopping in our stores." Craft fairs are useful for meeting buyers, other

Alyssa Levitan
Pin and Earrings (Handmade Papers Sculpted Around Stoneware/Porcelain with Stones and Beadwork)
See related information in Chapter 32
Photo: Dynamic Focus Photography
©1992

artisans, and checking out the competition and prices. Exceptional educational experiences are gained at fairs.

The Strictly Western shop displays special arts and crafts from the southwest, like a modern metal horse and a cow candlestick sculpture. Also tempting the tourists are bright-colored clothing such as hand-painted gauze broomstick skirts, handmade cotton blouses, and decorative hand-tooled western belts. The best-selling item, which is almost impossible to keep in stock, is mounted horns from Laredo longhorn cattle. Pictures of working ranches taken by a Dallas photographer line the walls of the shop. Showcases burst with dazzling jewelry from native-American New Mexico Indians.

Products for sale at these gift shops are purchased or received on consignment from several different marketing sources. Items are presented to Kathy Wood, either directly through the artisan, through sales representatives, or selected from the Dallas Market Center where hundreds of shops display merchandise for sale to buyers only. Periodically, she also discovers great items at various popular festivals held annually in the Dallas area, like Artfest or Canalfest. Most of the crafts are sold "exclusively" to the Loews Anatole, not because Wood requests this arrangement, but because sales through the gift shops are so considerable that most artisans have difficulty keeping up with demand.

"They (artisans) have to realize the retailer is going to have to double the price," Wood said. "A lot of people will come in and say, 'I think this price is great,' but you know you have to say, 'I have to double this.' They can sell it at a crafts fair for their cost, but when they sell to us at that same cost, we have to double it!" Everyone who wants to sell their work, from fine artists to the people who make country products, should seriously study their competition to make a realistic determination of an acceptable market price for their work.

Loews Anatole Hotel guests range from visiting cheerleaders to teachers attending job fairs to doctors, lawyers, and bankers attending conventions, so Wood tries "to keep a wide range of prices, something for everybody." Therefore, to accommodate the diverse preferences of these guests, price ranges vary at all of the shops. For instance, although most Four Corners Shop merchandise could be categorized as upper scale with items selling for hundreds of dollars, they also offer hand-painted eggs for only $2 apiece. Wood said that many guests ask, "Where is this made?" before buying. She continues, "It is real important, I think, to people that if they are buying something here, especially foreign visitors, and we do get a lot of foreign visitors, that it is made in this country."

CHAPTER 22

Calendars

*Calendars
Are
Guaranteed to
Attract
Attention
to Your Work*

PRODUCTS BUYERS WANT: arts and crafts

COSTS TO CONSIDER: Printing, sales, and distribution expenses. Costs from $25 on up.

One way to get your work onto walls in homes and offices and to enhance sales opportunities is to have a calendar printed that features your art or crafts. To celebrate 1993 as The Year of the American Craft, publisher Harry Abrams, Inc. produced a weekly appointment calendar. This calendar included vivid color images of selected crafts work accompanied by information about the national craft community and celebration events during this special year.

The Southern Highland Handicraft Guild published a calendar featuring the work of its various members. Each month featured a different artisan's work: enamel jewelry, ceramics, basketry, hand-woven apparel, ironwork, fiber art, woodturning, quilting, dulcimers, dollmakers, and woodcarving. Association members can help members try to find other artists who would also be interested in advertising work in this novel fashion.

Any art or craft guild, any group of contest winners, or any artist or craftsperson can create a calendar to help promote and sell work.

SPECIAL FEATURE: Calendars can be sold through thousands of potential retail outlets such as craft shops, galleries, museum stores, specialty shops, bookstores, and craft shows.

HOW TO CONTACT:

Write the Southern Highland Handicraft Guild for information about the guild's calendar:

Southern Highland Handicraft Guild
P.O. Box 9545
Asheville, North Carolina 28815

For information on the Calendar Marketing Association, contact:

Calendar Marketing Association
621 East Park Avenue
Libertyville, Illinois 60048
(708) 816-8660 or (800) 828-8225, or fax (708) 816-8662
Small calendar cards for wallets can be printed with a display photo of art or craft work. Contact printers for information on this process.

Since 1993, Winsor and Newton has held an annual competition that recognizes artists who use the company's art materials. Twelve talented artists are chosen for inclusion in a calendar; they submit two-dimensional work created in any medium (except photography) and of any subject. For information or an entry form, contact local art supply stores or consult artists' magazines, or contact:

Winsor and Newton Art Competition
P.O. Box 1396
Piscataway, New Jersey 08855-1396
(908) 562-0770

QUESTIONS TO ASK:

Do I want to underwrite all expenses on my own, or do I want to go in with a group on this printing project?
How much would a small calendar card cost?

CHAPTER 23

Profiting from Publicity

....

PRODUCTS BUYERS WANT: arts and crafts

....

COSTS TO CONSIDER: Mailing, some production, and possibly some outside editing help. Expect to pay at least $25 for self-publicity and at least $100 for outside consulting.

....

More than six hundred newspapers and eighty art magazines in the United States print stories about arts and crafts events of special interest to their readership. News about arts and crafts appeal to many people, thus artisans are already in a good position to attract a busy editor's attention. The practice of providing information of interest to editors should be regular and frequent. Newsworthy creativity will be rewarded with free publicity. If an artisan sends press releases that end up making the news regularly, then the notices being submitted are not only well written, but also of interest to the newspaper's readership. The ultimate goal of those seeking publicity is to have editors inviting them to submit information.

Press releases are excellent devices to generate publicity for artisan's work. Because a press release competes with many others for an editor's attention, it needs an interesting angle, a news "hook" that will grab the reader's attention. Decide what there is about this specific news item that warrants the public's undivided attention—something that will make an editor want to print the story. The primary goal should be to get the type of publicity that will stimulate customers to either make contact or buy products. This can be accomplished by regularly sending newsworthy press releases to the media.

SPECIAL FEATURE: Newspapers and magazines are always looking for worthwhile news and feature stories. Artisans should take advantage of the many kinds of publicity that can be generated at a minimal cost.

MAGAZINES:

Profitable Craft Merchandising
News Plaza
P.O. Box 1790
Peoria, Illinois 61614
(309) 682-6626
Distributed monthly for craft retailers, wholesalers, and manufacturers

Public Relations Journal
33 Irving Place
New York, New York 10003
(212) 995-2230
Focuses on publicity

NEWSLETTERS:

The Newsletter Yearbook Directory
The Newsletter Clearinghouse
44 West Market Street
P.O. Box 311
Rhinebeck, New York 12572

The Art of Self Promotion
  302 Garden Street
  Hoboken, New Jersey 07030
  This newsletter provides help for self-employed professionals with articles such as "Ten Slightly Unorthodox Ways to Promote Your Business," and "Do I Really Need a Brochure?" For a sample issue, send $1; a one-year subscription is $25.

DIRECTORIES

American Art Directory 1993-94
  R. R. Bowker
  121 Chanlon Road
  New Providence, New Jersey 07974
  This reference book provides a list of over six hundred newspapers and eighty art magazines and is available in many libraries.

Bacon's Information, Inc.
  332 South Michigan Avenue
  Chicago, Illinois 60604

Gebbie Press All-in-One Directory
  Box 1000
  New Paltz, New York 12561
  Gebbie Press lists names and addresses of daily and weekly newspapers, AM-FM radio stations, television stations, general consumer magazines, business papers, trade press, various ethnic-group presses, farm publications, and news syndicates in alphabetical order by category.

Editor and Publisher Publications
11 West 19th
New York, New York 10011
A directory that lists news and feature syndicates throughout the country providing information about columns. *Publicity Interview Directory* includes 3,800 magazine and newspaper editors, 1,840 radio stations, 725 TV stations, and 550 syndicated columnists.

Ulrich's International Periodicals Directory
R. R. Bowker
121 Chanlon Road
New Providence, New Jersey 07974
Updated quarterly, this book lists sixty-five thousand periodicals published from all over the world. Available in most libraries.

BOOKS

Publicity and Public Relations
Dorothy Doty
Barron's Educational Series
Hauppage, New York 11788

Getting Publicity: A Do-It-Yourself Guide for Small Business and Non-Profit Groups
Tana Fletcher
Self-Counsel Press
P.O. Box 12
Brookeville, Maryland 20833
This book tells how people can become an interview "source"—one of the experts whom journalists call when they're researching stories. It explains how to let the media know that you are available.

Publicity for Books and Authors
Peggy Glenn
Aames-Allen Publishing Company
1106 Main Street
Huntington Beach, California 92648
Inside information from an author who learned so much about promotion that she has built a successful book-publishing company.

Publicity Manual
Kate Kelly
Visibility Enterprises
450 West End Avenue
New York, New York 10024
This book contains tips, examples of press releases, and a comprehensive media resource list.

How to Write and Use Simple Press Releases That Work
Kate Kelly
Visibility Enterprises
450 West End Avenue
New York, New York 10024
Offers how-to guidelines, some samples of press releases, and a media resource directory. This is a condensation of her larger and more comprehensive *Publicity Manual*.

Marketing Made Easier—Guide to Free Product Publicity, 1993-1994
Barry Klein
Todd Publications
P.O. Box 301
West Nyack, New York 10994
More than one thousand magazines, newsletters and trade publications in one hundred twenty product categories make it easier to develop and administer a public relations campaign.

The TV News Handbook
William B. Becker
Insider's Guides
P.O. Box 2424
Southfield, Michigan 48037
This handbook tells how to get coverage on local TV stations.

TV Publicity Outlets Nationwide
P.O. Box 327
Washington Depot, Connecticut 06794
Single pages of this directory can be ordered if the artisan is only interested in promotion in specific cities.

The Unabashed Self-Promoter's Guide: What Every Man, Woman, Child and Organization in America Needs to Know about Getting Ahead by Exploiting the Media
Jeffrey Lant
Jeffrey Lant Associates, Inc.
50 Follen Street, Suite 507
Cambridge, Massachusetts 02138
This guide is loaded with ideas for no-cost/low-cost marketing of anything through the media.

Guerrilla P. R.
Michael Levine
HarperCollins Publishers, Inc.
10 East 53rd Street
New York, New York 10022
In addition to a wonderfully readable book, he includes a fantastic appendix listing of names and addresses of "Newspapers of National Significance," "Newspapers in Major Markets," the NATION'S TOP TWENTY "MAGAZINES," "Wire Services and Syndicates," "National Television News and Talk Shows," "Local TV Network Affiliates in Major Markets," and "Radio" networks.

The Publicity Handbook
  David Yale
  NTC Business Books
  Lincolnwood, Illinois 60646

Writer's Market
  Writer's Digest
  9933 Alliance Road
  Cincinnati, Ohio 45242
  (800) 289-0963
  Lists book and magazine markets, syndicates, contests and awards, plus writer's workshops.

Writing Effective News Releases
  Catherine V. McIntyre
  Piccadilly Books
  P.O. Box 25203
  Colorado Springs, Colorado 80936
  News release writing is the main topic of this book, which includes sample releases plus helpful hints on working with the media and how to create newsworthy ideas that immediately capture an editor's attention.

Do-It-Yourself Publicity
  David F. Ramacitti
  AMACOM
  A Division of American Management Association
  135 West 50th Street
  New York, New York 10020

Media services will write, then present stories of artists and craftspeople to newspapers, magazines, radio, and television stations around the country.

MEDIA SERVICES

Newspaper Feature Report
Bradley Communications
135 East Plumstead Avenue
Lansdowne, Pennsylvania 19050
(215) 259-1070
Designed to provide newspapers with a monthly assortment of camera-ready feature stories. Send $5 for a sample.

Washington News Service
440 National Press Building
Washington, D.C. 20045
For a fee, this service will deliver four hundred copies of a written press release to the Washington News Media estimated to reach one hundred million readers.

The Pocket Media Guide
307 West 36th Street
New York, New York 10018
For major media sources, order this free annual guide on your company letterhead.

Successful publicity releases utilize a format that is generally accepted and therefore appreciated by editors. Following is an example.

Contact: Janice West

           P.O. Box 156555

           Fort Worth, Texas 76155

           (817) 555-1234

**SAMPLE PRESS
RELEASE**

For immediate release

DENTON, TX. Marketing Your Arts and Crafts, a college course taught by Janice West, author of *Marketing Your Arts and Crafts*, will run in a four-class series at the University of North Texas beginning on March 21. The classes, which will run from 6:30 P.M. to 8:30 P.M. each night, will also be held on March 28, April 4, and April 11. For details, contact the University of North Texas, Center for Continuing Education and Conference Management, P.O. Box 5344, Denton, Texas 76203.

—30—

IMPORTANT INFORMATION ABOUT PRESS RELEASES

■ *Study local newspapers, regional, and national magazines at libraries.* Pay attention to the types of stories that are mentioned.

■ *Editors are interested in artists' upcoming exhibitions, major awards, honors, grants, and special events.*

■ *Be certain to include a contact name, phone number, and address.* This information can be placed at the end of the page or turned into a last one-sentence paragraph at the end.

■ *Place the most important information at the beginning.* The less critical material should be positioned toward the end, because editors may cut the last few sentences first.

■ *Press releases must be accurate.* The topic should be written clearly so that the subject can be easily understood by all readers.

■ *Simple English should be used in the written copy for the release.* Short sentences and short paragraphs make the release easier for readers to comprehend. Do not be surprised if the editor rewrites the release. This is standard procedure.

■ *Use 8½" x 11" paper.* Using letterhead stationary is acceptable.

■ *Always type a press release and double-space.* Avoid using a dot-matrix printer. Never send a photocopy. Photocopies label the sender as an amateur and immediately lose the editor's attention.

■ *Provide a 5" x 7" or 8" x 10" glossy black-and-white photo of the artist for newspapers, a 35mm color slide for magazines.* In the picture, the artist should preferably be interacting with his or her work, because an action shot is of much more interest to the public than a static photograph. However, there are times that a head shot and/or a picture of the work of art is more appropriate. Put name and address on the back of each photo sent. Do not use a pen or pencil! Use a sticker, taped label, or grease pencil instead. If photos are to be returned, then send a self-addressed, stamped envelope, but do not count on materials being returned because the media are so busy.

- *Always write in the third person.*

- *Add artist's quotes to the text.* Quotes enhance the credibility of the release.

- *Use action verbs.*

- *Use bullets whenever possible so that the release is easier to read.*

- *The copy should be proofed so that there are no spelling or grammatical errors.*

- *A self-addressed, stamped envelope (SASE) should be included, if the artist wants materials returned.*

- *Pay attention to deadlines.* A newspaper must have a press release at least two weeks in advance of the touted event. For magazines, three months is the usual lead time, but be certain to check with the editor.

- *Mail press releases.* It is not acceptable to deliver news releases in person.

- *Give a release date at the top of the page if a specific date is desired.* Give a "run no later than" or "kill" date for dated activities such as events.

- *Many times press releases generate enough interest in an artist for a newspaper or a magazine to do an article.* Be prepared for the additional questions that will be asked by a journalist.

- *The message in the press release needs to be beneficial to the public.*

- *Press releases can also be faxed.*

- *It is not necessary to have separate releases for all media.* The same release can be sent to print, radio, and television.

How to Work with Journalists/Writers

It feels like a dream. A journalist who has seen your work calls to schedule an interview. For all of thirty seconds, you are excited by the prospect of seeing your name in print. Then you start wondering what the writer expects. Anything an artisan can do to make a journalist's work easier will ensure not only that the story will be completed, but also that the artisan's professional, business-like attitude will be much appreciated and, consequently, remembered. The following suggestions will help the writer better know the artist and thereby facilitate understanding of the artistic work:

- *Prepare a complete write-up about all artistic work.* Update facts periodically to keep material current. Include dates of training, awards, prizes, shows—career highlights. Take special care when spelling complex terminology. Make the material as detailed as possible and be sure to explain any terms that might not be understood by the average reader.

- *Return all the writer's calls promptly.* Immediately identify yourself along with art or craft work. Be ready to respond to questions by having written materials nearby and in order.

- *Forward any promised material quickly.* Ask journalists what type of mailing they prefer. If one-day air necessitates that they must wait around all day to sign for the package, then two-day priority mail may be the better choice (and less expensive).

■ *Artists should include a self-addressed, stamped envelope with sufficient postage if they want materials returned.*

■ *Keep mailing receipts well organized.*

■ *Set up a separate file folder with every story previously written about artistic work.*

■ *Make a chart listing the date material was mailed, type of mailing used, and the date the material was received by the reporter.* If no receipt is requested by the mail carrier (as with return receipt), include a self-addressed, stamped postcard so that the journalist can easily provide notification that the materials have been received. If notification is not received within a reasonable time, generally seven days after the sender estimates that the package should have been delivered, then make a quick call to the journalist to verify that all materials were received in good condition. Ask if he has developed any additional questions after reviewing the package.

■ *Package materials carefully.* Transparencies and slides should be clearly labeled with name of work and dimensions, then placed between cardboard for protection.

■ *Be careful with originals.* Send copies of all materials unless there is no concern that originals be returned. Realize that the journalist loses control over all work when he mails the items to the newspaper or magazine publisher. It is impossible for him to keep track of work once submitted. Do not expect the writer to make copies for you!!! Most are on tight deadlines and limited monetary budgets.

■ *Be prepared.* Do not wait until the last minute to prepare or send materials. Professional artists learn to allow for problems and delays. Meet all deadlines for sending materials. Missing agreed-upon deadlines will be regarded as inconsiderate and unprofessional behavior.

■ *Be early for any scheduled interviews.* Allow enough time to find the location of the meeting. Arriving a few minutes early will give the interviewee time to review notes or do a few deep-breathing exercises.

- *Make a list.* Journalists especially appreciate receiving material that teaches their readers facts in an entertaining yet simple manner. Lists of tips are especially popular.

- *When concluding a meeting or telephone conversation with a writer, be sure to make it easy for the writer to reapproach the interviewee if necessary.* Joei Skesfington of the Crafters Showcase in Paramus, New Jersey, concludes her telephone conversations by adding, "If you have any more questions or want to talk, feel free to call back." This congenial attitude makes it easy for the interviewer to reestablish contact.

- *When talking about providing information to a writer, artists should not say that they have been too busy to collect and send their finest material, have a bio picture taken, or have 35mm slides prepared.*

- *If a call to a journalist is deemed necessary, be sure to start the conversation by asking, "Is this a good time for you to talk?" or "Are you on deadline?"* Then get to the point. Be considerate of the journalist's time.

- *It is common practice especially with print journalists to ask if they have received your press release.*

- *Artists should avoid comments that lead the journalist to believe that cooperation on the writing project is low on their list of priorities.* This type of comment might motivate the reporter to write about another artist who does know how to cooperate. If an artist desires publicity, every effort must be made to promptly provide all requested materials.

Artists who are serious about promoting their work should begin collecting materials that will promote their careers. The following materials should be prepared in advance and be ready for distribution at a moment's notice:

- artist's bio (include documentation from past shows, awards, or other types of professional recognition)

- artist's bio photo—either black-and-white photo or 35mm slide

- labeled transparencies with gray bar and/or color scale

- written description of transparencies including dimensions

- press release

- clips from published articles

- artist's statement (optional)

There are few opportunities to receive free career-enhancing publicity. The equivalent, if purchased, could cost thousands of dollars in paid advertising. Try to take advantage of all such occasions. If the advantages of cooperating with a journalist are ever doubted, compare the benefits of the free publicity with the cost of having to pay for magazine and newspaper advertising. Remember, the more times potential buyers see artists' names in print, the more favorably they will regard their work.

CHAPTER 24

Construction Projects

There Are Big Bucks in Selling to Major Construction Projects

PRODUCTS BUYERS WANT: Those pertinent to large commissions. They usually want an artist or craftsperson capable of handling massive projects, such as sizable murals.

COSTS TO CONSIDER: *Sales Prospector*
Year's subscription to all U.S. regional editions: $1,925
Year's subscription for twenty-four issues of one edition: $386
Two-month trial subscription (four issues): $68

Sales Prospector is a semimonthly newsletter listing timely information on major construction projects planned around the country. The newsletter covers fourteen regions of the United States and all of Canada in fifteen separate editions. Listings give contact information for the contracting corporation and the architect, if available. Projects cited include schools, hospitals, hotels, institutions, retail complexes, office buildings, cultural facilities, and manufacturing plants. Since the newsletter is produced for the whole range of contract construction services, new military training grounds and munitions factories are also included.

One example of a large commissioned project was in 1978, when Mara Smith of Denton, Texas, created a series of five murals in the massive brick walls of the Loews Anatole Hotel. Over 252,000 pounds of clay were used to form one thousand wet bricks, which were then grided, carved, numbered, dried for one month, then fired to exhibit carvings named The World Tree, North Star, Saguaro del Sur, Daydreaming About a Modern City, and Unicorn of Destiny.

SPECIAL FEATURE: can locate building and construction projects anywhere in the United States and Canada

---

HOW TO CONTACT: Details available from:
Sales Prospector
751 Main Street
P.O. Box 9079
Waltham, Massachusetts 02154-9079
(617) 899-1271, or fax (617) 899-2546

QUESTIONS TO ASK: Would several people I know benefit from ordering this newsletter so that the cost could be divided?
Is this publication available through local libraries?

Selling to Professionals

*Selling
Your Arts
and Crafts
to Professional
Captive
Audiences*

....

PRODUCTS BUYERS WANT: arts and crafts

....

COSTS TO CONSIDER: mailing expenses, from about $30 on up

....

Many professionals collect artwork for the personal enjoyment of being surrounded by special, beautiful objects and for display purposes in their offices. The collector certainly regards any appreciation of the art as a plus. Often the good-investment factor gains commissions resulting in additional work for the artist. Another way to take advantage of a captive audience is to arrange to hold an exhibit in the office of a doctor, attorney, insurance agent, or real estate broker. A veterinarian has even participated in sponsoring such exhibitions.

Judy Gibson, a native of Paris, Texas, works in a wide range of media from oils to watercolor. Her subject matter varies from realistic portrayals of bluebonnets to exquisitely detailed equine art. Gibson's commissioned artwork has been prominently displayed in the lobby of Peoples National Bank. She has had a one-person show at InterFirst Bank and NCNB (NationsBank), also located in Paris, Texas.

Be on the lookout for temporary exhibition spaces. One artist makes it a policy to ask business owners if they would be interested in allowing him to show his work every time he spots a blank wall where his art could be displayed.

Often, businesses will really appreciate artists' inquiries. They have found that their customers and clients enjoy having fine artwork to view.

SPECIAL FEATURES: Selling to professionals assures continuing sales to virtually an infinite market, good possibilities for word-of-mouth sales, and referrals to the exhibitor's associates and friends. Displays provide direct exposure for your art and craft work, especially when exhibited in professional offices or lobbies.

HOW TO CONTACT: Look under listings such as physicians, dentists, Realtors, and attorneys in the *Yellow Pages*. At the library, copy information from *Who's Who* and other biographical directories; addresses and phone numbers are often included. If there are any problems with locating reference material, ask the librarian. Write the professionals, enclosing a business card and pictures of your work along with a price list. Include a self-addressed, stamped envelope to make it easier for a response.

QUESTIONS TO ASK: Would you be interested in seeing brochures, slides or a sample of my artwork? Do you know of any exhibitions being held in private offices?

Guy M. Michaels
Handcarved Pink Alabaster Vase
Fused with Maple, Ebony and
Cocobolo Woods
See related information in
Chapter 32
Photo: Dynamic Focus Photography
©1992

CHAPTER 26

The Sculpture Source

*Now—
for
the First
Time—
Sell Sculpture
by Computer
Imaging*

PRODUCTS BUYERS WANT: sculpture (in all media categories)

COSTS TO CONSIDER: sculpture source membership:
individual level member: $55
associate level member: $100
professional level member: $250

"Have you ever heard of optical disc recording?, because presenting large-screen high-resolution video images is a free benefit of membership," says Josef Marker, spokesman for the International Sculpture Center (ISC), based in Washington, D.C. ISC operates Sculpture Source, an international, computerized Visual Artists Registry and referral service. ISC categorizes sculptors' works from submitted slides, then compiles a list of artists for referral to interested buyers. "Associate-level members receive up to six free images, and professional-level members receive up to nine free images as part of their membership benefit package," Marker says. (Individual-level members are allowed up to three free images.)

Although twenty-six artists on the Washington, D.C., slide registry are from foreign countries (individual-level membership for overseas participants is $70), most are American.

These images are transferred to optical disc for three dimensional computer-

Sherry Henderson
"Legend of the Horse" (Bronze)
See related information in
Chapter 33
Photo: Sherry Henderson

ized showings to clientele, which includes art consultants, curators, collectors, gallery owners, architects, government agencies, public art coordinators, and corporations. The ISC also uses Sculpture Source as one of its primary sources when considering artists for its own exhibitions.

The ISC, working as a nonprofit organization, refers sculptors worldwide, but most clients are from the northeast U.S. corridor and mid-Atlantic states. Various organizations, such as UNICEF, feature works from Sculpture Source artists in their traveling international exhibits.

SPECIAL FEATURES: Membership includes subscriptions to *Sculpture* magazine and *Sculpture Maquette,* which provide international listings of grants, competitions, scholarships, fellowships, group rates on health and studio insurance, residencies and calls for artists, discounts at foundries and art suppliers, and discount rates on hotel and car rental.

Membership also includes special rates and priority registration for the ISC's biennial sculpture conferences—acclaimed worldwide as the largest, most diverse meetings on contemporary sculpture. Internationally known presenters conduct panel discussions, seminars, and workshops.

Additionally, trade fairs, tours of public art and artists' studios, community exhibitions, and special events are offered.

HOW TO CONTACT: Details are available from Sculpture Source:
International Sculpture Center
1050 17th Street N.W.
Suite 250
Washington, D.C. 20036
(202) 785-1144, or fax (202) 785-0810

QUESTIONS TO ASK: What are the requirements of membership?
What are the various benefits of membership?
Do you have any literature about Sculpture Source to send me?

CHAPTER 27

The National Museum of Women in the Arts

A Museum Dedicated to Presenting Art of Emerging Women Artists

PRODUCTS BUYERS WANT: fine arts and fine crafts by women artists. To be included in the Library and Research Center, artists must have had at least one solo exhibition.

COSTS TO CONSIDER: Submission of slides/transparencies for the Library and Research Center. This costs $25 and up.

Since 1987, the historic Renaissance Revival building that houses the National Museum of Women in the Arts (NMWA) has attracted thousands of people from around the globe to view the single most important collection of art by women in the world. Every month, more visitors are discovering this national treasure containing a permanent collection that presents artwork by over five hundred women artists from the sixteenth century to the present. Their extraordinary collection includes paintings, drawings, sculpture, pottery, prints, books, and photography beginning with early works such as *Holy Family with St. John* by Renaissance artist Lavinia Fontana. The extensive collection ranges from floral still lives by Rachel Ruysch to prints by Mary Cassatt. Sculpture by Camille Claudel, the true sculptor of many of the bronzes originally attributed to Auguste Rodin, and photographs by Louise

Dahl-Wolfe are featured, along with many other brilliant, but often underappreciated artists.

Others well known in this collection include Elisabeth Vigée-Le Brun, Audry Flack, Rosa Bonheur, Georgia O'Keeffe, Frida Kahlo, Lee Krasner, Helen Frankenthaler, and Alma Thomas. The NMWA has significant special collections, such as over one hundred silver objects crafted by eighteenth-century women silversmiths.

The innovative State Chapter/State Exhibit Program of the National Museum of Women in the Arts has been launched to give women artists from all over the country the chance to bring their diverse artistic visions to a national audience. Already artists from Colorado, Kansas, New York, North Carolina, Texas, and Washington have participated in this new program.

The Library and Research Center houses the world's largest specialized collection of the artwork of women artists. The museum's literary holdings include over eight thousand volumes of reference books, plus monographs, rare publications, artists' books and special collections, like the library of American abstractionist Irene Rice Pereira.

Additionally, the Library and Research Center maintains resource files on over thirteen thousand women artists from all periods and nationalities. These files include the work of contemporary artists who have had at least one solo exhibition. The museum actively organizes a wide variety of workshops, symposia, and educational programs for children. They have also initiated a program of art tours in the United States and Europe.

The museum gift shop displays special gifts, wearable art, and art for the home. Artist Kim Smith's designs, sterling silver earrings and pins depicting architectural and interior details of the museum's landmark building, are featured.

Rebecca Phillips Abbott, NMWA administration, says that "although nearly fifty percent of all practicing artists in the United States today are women, 95 percent to 98 percent of the works in our nation's art museums are by men." NMWA's main goal is to develop a voice for the much-deserved recognition of history's great women artists. After all, she points out, it is the work of American Impressionist Lilla Cabot Perry that still hangs in Monet's home in home in Giverny, even though Perry's superb works are rarely seen exhibited in America's museums.

SPECIAL FEATURES: NMWA's special exhibitions present women's artistic accomplishments in an innovative manner. The museum sponsors several exhibitions series, such as its State Exhibitions of regional art, which is displayed in the Gudelsky State Gallery. International shows are offered on a rotating schedule. NMWA's "Forefront" series presents the art of emerging and midcareer women artists.

HOW TO CONTACT:

The National Museum of Women in the Arts is situated in downtown Washington, D.C., at the corner of New York Avenue and 13th Street, N.W.—convenient to public transportation—one block north of Metro Center. The White House and Convention Center are within easy walking distance. For more information, contact:

The National Museum of Women in the Arts

1250 New York Avenue, N.W.
Washington, D.C. 20005-3920
(202) 783-5000

QUESTIONS TO ASK:

How do I contact the museum's Coordinator of State Programs for information? Can you send me literature about The National Museum of Women in the Arts?

Dennis Kappeler
Front of Union Station
Photo: Dennis Kappeler

CHAPTER 28

America! Stores

*Customers
Really Do Want
to Buy
American
Products*

PRODUCTS BUYERS WANT:	arts and crafts made in America
COSTS TO CONSIDER:	long-distance telephone charges, starting at about $10

America! stores feature gift items made in the United States. Flags, jewelry, and desk accessories are but a few of the thousands of items lining the shelves of one of the most interesting shops in Virginia. These stores overflow with keepsakes made by all types of artists and crafters. Buyers for the stores gravitate to items with a patriotic theme, such as eye-catching, colorful banners designed to capture attention at the office, trade show booths, or county fairs. "America the Beautiful" afghans, woven with fine naturally grown fibers, vie for attention with patriotic linens (towels, oven mitts, potholders, napkins, and place mats) in red, white, and blue, topped off by bright stars—all great for election parties, country homes, or barbecues. This type of merchandise is especially popular with travelers because it can be carried home so easily in one of the store's hand-crafted "I Love My Country" totes.

Jane Crawford, owner of the three America! stores and the catalog company, says that the store buyers are also interested in providing products that represent Native America and the West. Many of their artistic items and crafts are "exclusives," so they can be found only in America! stores or catalogs.

SPECIAL FEATURE: This special store boasts that every item they carry is "Made in the USA." Currently there are three retail stores: America! (118 King Street, Alexandria, Virginia; and Pentagon City Mall, Arlington, Virginia), Made in America! (Union Station, 50 Massachusetts Avenue, N.E., Washington, D.C.), and a catalog titled America!

HOW TO CONTACT:

America!
118 King Street
Alexandria, Virginia 22314
(703) 836-1491

QUESTIONS TO ASK:

Can you send me the America! catalog?
How should I submit my work to your store(s) for consideration?
How are sales through America! handled? Outright purchase? Consignment?

Owner of the America! Stores

"There is some neat stuff here, really neat stuff!" an enthusiastic teenage boy loudly whispers as he confides to his buddy. They are both inspecting the cache of miniature soldiers displayed in fighting positions inside a glass case at America! located in Old Town Alexandria's Small Mall in Virginia. His companion nods, unwilling to divert his attention from the rows of miniature soldiers in blue or gray regalia. They both stoop down to get a good look at a lower shelf where General Custer presides over tiny calvary men battling the Sioux. Artist Ron Wall forged these fine-quality pewter military miniatures. Each meticulously hand-painted soldier, flag bearer, and horseman is not only signed with Ron Wall's trademark W, but also bears the date of the original sculpture on the base.

"We opened five years ago," explains Jane Crawford, owner and buyer for America!, "at about the same time that the textile industry began advertising 'Made in America.' We thought that maybe the public would appreciate a source for American products." Crawford's assessment of American tastes hit their intended target. After experiencing success in Old Town Alexandria, they opened a second store called Made in America! in the main hall of historic Union Station in Washington, D.C., a third America! store in popular Pentagon City Mall, and recently began distribution of full-color America! catalogs designed to meet the needs of both individuals and corporations. Will they continue to open more America! stores? Crawford admits that "we're always thinking about growing."

Although tourists find the three metropolitan stores convenient, Crawford expects to reach a bigger audience for their American-made products through their catalogs, which advertise only items that are "crafted with pride in the USA." Additionally, Crawford explains they are anxious to "do a lot of work with corporations and international travelers."

Items such as the U.S. flags featured by the company have become quite popular with corporate clientele. All flags are available in two popular sizes: the four-inch-by-six-inch rayon flags mounted on a ten-inch ebonized black staff with gilt spear designed to sit on tables, and the three-foot-by-five-foot, residential-size flags constructed of durable nylon fabric appropriate for outdoor display. Several popular styles are offered, such as the all-time-favorite fifty-star U.S. flag hanging along with other, more unusual examples: famous flags such as the Betsy Ross, the First Navy Jack, the POW/MIA flag, and Democratic and Republican flags.

Discerning buyers often gravitate to the intricately engraved items. Polished-pewter accessories offered in different price ranges are perfect for gift-giving occasions, from saying thanks to retirement farewells. Pewter beverage coolers, pencil cups, or jewelry boxes can be engraved with the initials or names of the recipient, alongside the U.S. Seal.

Foreign visitors usually express interest in items that personify their concept of American tradition. So miniature pewter statues from the Chilmark Collection titled *Robert E. Lee, Pickett's Charge,* and *Brother Against Brother* sell well. Framed reissues of pre-1939 tobacco cards with General Joe Johnston and General Benjamin F. Butler tempt foreign collectors. A limited-edition eagle sculpture cast in genuine bronze by world-renowned sculptor Mark Hopkins perches on a nearby shelf. Fun items like "stolen towels" from the White House or French-milled soap with the U.S. Great Seal add presidential presence to bathrooms located anywhere in the world.

Guests will be impressed when desserts are served on unforgettable White House plates with matching cups and saucers—accurate reproductions of the china patterns used in the White House during the presidential administrations of Washington, Jefferson, Adams, Pierce, Madison, or Jackson. Each president's favorite dessert recipe is included in formal blue gift boxes along with certificates of authenticity. After-dinner coffee can be served to guests on elegant ebony trays designed by Couroc, who combines ancient techniques of cloisonné, oriental paper cutting, and metal inlay.

For the child at heart, old-time wooden "Alphabet Blocks" where an apple tree stands for "A," a red heart represents "H," and the moon depicts "M" can be selected. Rosalie, the artist who produces the blocks, explains, "During the 1850s, wooden blocks and pull toys were produced using lithograph prints applied to wood. Inspired by that idea, my original watercolor prints are applied to the wood as they were done in the 1850s. We have aged and tattered them to appear old and once loved by a child of yesterday."

Coasters, ornaments, cups, and adorned bells with the pineapple friendship symbol captivate collectors. Brass insignias branding candles with the pineapple (state symbol of Virginia) or the cardinal (the state bird) provide indelible reminders of the Old Dominion state. Rose-scented soap from Carter's Grove Plantation near Williamsburg is wrapped with paper that describes the eighteenth-century plantation overlooking the James River. For homesick visitors, other states are represented in small plastic-wrapped packages of soil labeled Land-by-the-Inch from states such as Arkansas, California, Hawaii, Kentucky, Nebraska, New Mexico, and Vermont.

Political paraphernalia represents both parties equally. Infant's "Wee"-publican and "Demi"-crat T-shirts are available for those who want children to express party loyalty at an early age. Red, white, and blue boxer shorts may be selected by those who prefer to keep patriotic preference under cover. Stars and stripes bandannas are appropriate for man and dog alike. "America the Beautiful" afghans, woven with only the finest natural grown fibers, will keep any patriot warm on winter nights. Heads will rest comfortably on navy wool pillows embroidered richly in gold with Old Glory or the federal eagle. Democrat or Republican watches keep politically correct time.

Crawford emphasizes the fact that several designs sold in their stores are represented by them exclusively. "Buyers can find anything at our store, with prices ranging from fifteen cents to fine-art objects priced at several hundred dollars," Crawford says. "We wanted a retail concept that offered the public an opportunity to buy gifts made in America."

CHAPTER 29

Resources for Artists with Disabilities

Attract Collectors to Your Artwork!

PRODUCTS BUYERS WANT:	work by visual artists with physical disabilities
COSTS TO CONSIDER:	slides: at least $25

Artists with physical disabilities often face many obstacles that severely limit their exhibition opportunities. With limited accessibility to numerous galleries and unfavorable attitudes toward persons with disabilities such as impaired hearing, speech, vision, or mobility, talented artists find that their opportunities to compete equally with able-bodied artists can be adversely affected.

As its promotional literature states, Resources for Artists with Disabilities "promotes public awareness of, and exhibition opportunities for, professional visual artists with physical disabilities." Exhibits at New York University, the Tweed Gallery at the New York City Hall, and the Lobby Gallery at the Jacob Javits Federal Office Building in New York City have offered the public direct access to these talented artists' work. Additionally, symposiums such as "Women Artists—Disabled" at the Museum of Modern Art and "Art Despite Physical Disabilities" at the Donnell Library Center in New York have been held. A thirty-minute video documentary has been produced where three physically disabled women artists discuss slides of their art, the life experiences that have influenced their work, as well as the impact of their physical disabilities upon their creative processes.

Artists with disabilities who wish to participate in any of the following activities should send slides of their artwork along with a brief description of themselves or a resumé to:

Resources for Artists With Disabilities
77 Seventh Avenue
Suite PhG
New York, New York 10011-6645

■ Resources organizes approximately three open-invitational shows per year. This entails finding the exhibition spaces, as well as coordinating a jury of art authorities who select work from submitted slides.

■ Resources distributes information received about exhibition opportunities and appropriate competitions to all artists on their mailing list.

■ Resources will advise artists about preparation of slides or portfolios for presentation to galleries or museums.

■ Resources accepts three to ten 35mm slides of artwork for permanent placement in its slide collection. Each slide must be labeled with artist's name, title of piece, dimensions, medium, and year executed. (Please send slides in an envelope with cardboard for protection.)

■ Resources distributes press information about its activities to arts organizations, disability organizations, and to the general press.

SPECIAL FEATURE: Artists with physical disabilities are encouraged to send, along with their resumé, appropriately labeled slides of their artwork for inclusion in a slide archive that is available for viewing by exhibiting directors and curators. Send materials to:

Resources for Artists with Disabilities, Inc.
77 Seventh Avenue
Suite PhG
New York, New York 10011-6645
(212) 691-5490

For information published by a support group for disabled professional visual artists, contact:
Disabled Artists' Network
P.O. Box 20781
New York, New York 10025

Will my disability qualify me for access to Resources?
How many people generally review the slide archives per year?
What organizations and publications receive press information from Resources?

QUESTIONS TO ASK:

CHAPTER 30

The National Trust

*Lavish
Locations
Looking to Buy
American
Products*

PRODUCTS BUYERS WANT: arts and crafts made in America

COSTS TO CONSIDER: Cost of long-distance telephone, samples, and shipping. Figure on about $25 or more.

What awaits tourists after they visit the famous Gardens of Filoli, which were featured on both the television serial "Dynasty" as well as the movie *Heaven Can Wait*? A fabulous gift shop beckons, where visitors can spend as much time and money as they like buying arts and crafts. This shop sells over one million dollars in merchandise every year.

"We have no set policy because our museums are so diverse," says Tom Roberts of the merchandising division at the National Trust. "Our nation's National Trust for Historic Preservation operates seventeen famous historical properties located from New York to California. Our needs change daily based on inventory," "However, we try to talk to everyone."

Roberts usually shops the major craft shows, especially those held in Philadelphia, Baltimore, and Washington, D.C. He says anyone interested in selling through the National Trust properties should feel free to "call the switchboard at the National Trust and the operator will put them in touch with the right people. I always enjoy talking to people. We'll want to see a sample and hear why it should be included. Brochures are not necessary."

SPECIAL FEATURE: Most National Trust properties are open every day throughout the year, closing only for the observance of major holidays.

ALPHABETICAL LISTING OF NATIONAL TRUST PROPERTIES (WITH YEARS BUILT)

Belle Grove (1794) in Middletown, Virginia

Brucemore (1885) in Cedar Rapids, Iowa

Casa Amesti Adobe (1834) in Monterey, California

Chesterwood (1898) in Stockbridge, Massachusetts

Cliveden (1763-1767) in Philadelphia, Pennsylvania

Cooper-Molera Adobe (1830) in Monterey, California

Decatur House (1819) in Washington, D.C.

Drayton Hall (1738-42) in Charleston, South Carolina

Filoli (1916) in Woodside, California

Frank Lloyd Wright Home and Studio (1889) in Oak Park, Illinois

Lyndhurst (1838 and 1864-65) in Tarrytown, New York

Montpelier (1755) in Orange, Virginia

Oatlands (1800) in Leesburg, Virginia

Pope-Leighey House (1940) in Alexandria, Virginia

Shadows-on-the-Teche (1831-1834) in New Iberia, Louisiana

Woodlawn Plantation (1800-1803) in Alexandria, Virginia

Woodrow Wilson House (1915) in Washington, D.C.

HOW TO CONTACT:

American artists or crafters can contact:

National Trust for Historic Preservation
Merchandising Division
1785 Massachusetts Avenue, N.W.
Washington, D.C. 20036
(202) 673-4000

QUESTIONS TO ASK:

What kind of samples are you most interested in examining?

How long after submission before I find out if the National Trust is interested in acquiring my work?

Will I know which National Trust gift shop sells my work?

Proper Product Packaging

According to the July 1991 issue of *The Crafts Report*, Tim Bissett, an artist in Calgary, readily admits to being a perfectionist. That is how he has quickly become an established presence in the Western Canadian gallery scene, by paying extraordinary attention to proper presentation of his Far Eastern raku artwork. Early in his career, Tim discovered that successful packaging design means more than using just any container. His search to showcase his expensive ceramic pieces finally ended once he located a guitar maker. The guitar maker now painstakingly constructs custom Baltic birch boxes with brass clasps and hinges for the artisan's exquisite ceramics. Less costly pieces lay tucked in black tissue inside red cardboard boxes deftly tied with gold cord. Tim Bissett advises artists to totally personalize everything they make.

Every artist faces the problem of how to package artwork to enhance its appeal for the retailer and, ultimately, the customer. Attention should be given to special events and holiday themes whenever possible. Consider packaging arts and crafts creatively to reflect the different events. Decorate display items in festive holiday themes. Gift-wrap products in colorful holiday papers such as red and green for the Christmas season. Add miniature flags to packages for the Fourth of July or tiny red hearts for Valentine's Day. These decorative add-ons need not be expensive. Special items and theme packaging attract customers' attention, thus encouraging them to buy.

Other special occasions and holidays to plan for as part of a merchandising effort are Mother's Day, Easter, Halloween, First Communion, Hanukkah, New Year's, Labor Day, Weddings, Father's Day, New Baby, Anniversaries, St. Patrick's Day, Back-to-School, Thanksgiving, President's Day, Elections, Graduation, and Birthdays.

Andrew and Pat Brazington are confident that sellers will realize the importance of Afrocentric gift-wrap. In 1990, they founded Ethnic Reams, Rolls, and Bags. This Dallas company is partial to designs in the black liberation colors of red, black, and green. Wrapping paper and bags can be supplied for all important celebrations including Kwanzaa, an African-American festival commemorating the traditional African harvest.

Product containers range from plastic garment bags to paper bags, from cardboard boxes to huge wooden crates, and many variations in between. Consider the following hints:

1. *Packaging sells the product.* The customer will examine the package longer if it is attractive and appealing.

2. *Packaging must identify the product.* Whether the container is imprinted by hand or by machine, the contents should be readily discerned.

3. *If the container is constructed of transparent material, then the item inside will be promptly revealed.*

4. *If the product cannot be viewed as a complete unit by the customer, then the picture on the package has to do the selling.*

5. *If possible, have the container imprinted with company name, logo, and address.* This is why retailers have messages printed on that great sales tool more commonly known as the shopping bag.

6. *Put forth effort to have a design, color, or logo carried through in all the tools of sale such as business cards, stationery, and packaging.*

7. *Make sure the contents are safeguarded by a sturdy container that provides protection from any external elements such as the cold, heat, water, or careless handling.*

8. *Many suppliers, such as Designer Paper Products in Yonkers, New York, use recycled paper as often as possible.*

Thus, when considering the best way to package artwork, take into account safety, simplicity, appeal, cost effectiveness, and the environment. Remember that customers' first impressions are important. Proper packaging will tell a lot about the product, but even more about the artisan's attitude toward the business side of his craft. To acquire more information about various types of packaging materials, contact the following:

For information about Afrocentric wrapping paper and gift bags to celebrate all occasions from christenings to Christmas, contact:

Ethnic Reams, Rolls, and Bags

605 North Vernon Avenue
Dallas, Texas 75208
(214) 946-3772

To order giftware or jewelry boxes, shopping bags, totes, tissue paper, metallic foil wrapping paper, holiday merchandise bags, and paper with holiday themes. For free samples, contact:

Designer Paper Products, Inc.

45 Prospect Street
Yonkers, New York 10701
(800) 831-7791

For all kinds of bags (shopping, garment), boxes (apparel, giftware, jewelry), tissue (white, colored, patterned), ribbons, bows, tape, tags, recycled perforated bubble paper, hangers, contact:

The NU-ERA Group, Inc.

727 North Eleventh Street
St. Louis, Missouri 63101-9806
(800) 325-7073 or fax (314) 231-3917
Accepts major credit cards.

To order gift, floral, boutique, jewelry, or tin boxes or to request catalog, contact:

U.S. Box Corporation
  1296 McCarter Highway
  Newark, New Jersey 07104
  (718) 387-1510 or (201) 481-2000

To order bags (garment, paper, plastic, shopping, zip-lock), boxes (giftware, hat, holiday, jewelry), gift wrap, imprinted labels, ribbon, tissue paper, yarn or other packaging materials, contact:

Robert H. Ham Associates, Ltd.
  P.O. Box 77398
  Greensboro, North Carolina 27417
  (800) 334-6965, or fax (800) 832-6775

For a free catalog of made-to-order boxes, tape, packing supplies, colored, white, waxed tissue, or shredded newspaper, contact:

Springfield Corrugated Box Company, Inc.
  P.O. Box 714
  74 Moylan Lane
  Agawam, Massachusetts 01001
  (800) 437-8453 or (413) 789-2268, or fax (413) 789-2313

To order boxes and crates for retail display or gift packaging (silk-screening is available for custom lid decoration), contact:

AFTOSA
  1034 Ohio Avenue
  Richmond, California 94804
  (800) 231-0397
  Accepts major credit cards

To show off your handiwork in bags that are ideal for handcrafted items and perfect for odd-shaped, fragile or heavy products, contact:

Action Bag Company

501 North Edgewood Avenue

Wood Dale, Illinois 60191

(800) 824-BAGS, or in Illinois (708) 766-2881

To order mailing tubes, contact:

Zazoo Mills, Inc.

P.O. Box 369

New Oxford, Pennsylvania 17350

(800) 242-5216, or fax (717) 624-4420

PACKAGING MATERIALS

Kristina Beckman
Birch Wreath with Freeze Dried
Flowers
See related information in
Chapter 32
Photo: Dynamic Focus Photography
©1993

Artrider Shows

*Special
Places
to Sell
Special
Crafts*

PRODUCTS BUYERS WANT: arts and crafts made in America

COSTS TO CONSIDER: slides, booth rental, and travel. Plan to pay
at least $500.

Artrider Productions works to locate show sites in affluent, crafts-conscious markets. They promote high-quality retail crafts fairs at sites renowned for their beauty or historical significance. According to their literature, shows are always unique in both character and scope, but all maintain the highest standards of craftsmanship, organization, and professionalism.

In 1993, two new events in the affluent Philadelphia market premiered. Crafts at Glen Foerd, set in a magnificent historic estate built in the 1850s in suburban Philadelphia, is held in April or May. In December, the Pennsylvania Crafts Fair is conducted at the newly constructed Pennsylvania Convention Center in the heart of Philadelphia's historic Center City. The architects of this "state of the art" building plan to have this be the finest facility of its kind in the nation. Spring and Fall Crafts at Lyndhurst, which overlooks the Hudson River, is held annually in May in Tarrytown, New York. This mansion, designed in the Gothic revival style, is one of the most influential romantic structures built in America. Other shows are administered during the year at the Morristown

Armory in New Jersey and Crafts Park Avenue located on Manhattan's spectacular Upper East Side.

SPECIAL FEATURE: Artrider Productions works to maintain high standards of craftsmanship at every show. Only handmade American crafts are accepted.

HOW TO CONTACT: **Artrider Productions Inc.**
4 Deming Street
Woodstock, New York 12498
(914) 679-7277

QUESTIONS TO ASK: How many exhibitors will be at the shows?
How much is the booth rental?
What portions of my booth will be furnished?
Are tables and chairs available for rent?
What kind of security is provided?
Are electrical outlets available?

Business Cards

PRODUCTS BUYERS WANT: arts and crafts

COSTS TO CONSIDER: ranges from $15 up

Business cards should be planned, designed, and dispersed liberally. This is the next best means to advertising arts and crafts, aside from a customer actually seeing an artisan's work. Art and craft work can be interestingly depicted by photograph, pen-and-ink, or some other equally noticeable method. When designing business cards, consider whether or not the card is easy-to-read and eye-catching. Be creative. For instance, glass artisans might print their cards on see-through plastics; jewelry makers can use papers that resemble marble or malachite; woodworkers can print on thin balsa wood. A collectible card will make people remember arts and crafts products! Consider the following suggestions:

- *Use color for emphasis.* Colored inks often cost the same as black ink, yet they invariably attract more attention.

- *Consider fold-over cards.* Die-cut cards can illustrate work by having the card shaped to the design of a product.

- *Make cards rolodex ready.* When cards are custom-made for files, they create a handy reference for potential clients.

■ *Use standard size for business cards.* Be sure that cards are the standard 2"x 3½" size. Odd-sized cards will not fit into wallets, so they tend to get thrown away.

■ *Use all of the card.* Use the front and back of each card, perhaps drawing a map to a studio, gallery, or outlet on the reverse side. List special services. Highlight major awards, exhibitions, or achievements. Create a lasting impression!

■ *Make the card easy to read.* Use vivid color contrasts, letters that are large enough, and clearly understood typefaces. Wording should be legible.

■ *Consider photo cards.* These cards feature a color picture of the artist or artistic work.

SPECIAL FEATURE: Business cards are more than just a way of providing potential customers with a name, address, and phone number. Cards should create distinctive images for individual businesses, thus helping to sell arts and crafts.

HOW TO CONTACT: Printing shops in every town can supply business cards, stationery, and various other paper supplies. Look in the *Yellow Pages* for those located nearby. If mail order is more appealing, try contacting one of the following companies. Several offer toll-free numbers and free catalogs or samples of their work.

For a free catalog of all types of business stationery items such as letterhead, envelopes, postcards, business cards (including artist's sketch designs with studio or craft items in pen-and-ink), and labels, contact:

The Business Book
One East Eight Avenue
Oshkosh, Wisconsin 54906-0002
(800) 558-0220, or fax (414) 426-1132

Bucher Brothers supplies business cards and "mini stickers" in satin gold or silver. Offers free samples and brochures. Contact:

Bucher Brothers
729 Leo Street
Dayton, Ohio 45404
(513) 228-2022

Color Q prints business cards incorporating photos and postcard reproductions of art. Offers free art kit with paper samples and helpful hints on marketing prints. Contact:

Color Q
2710 Dryden Road
Dayton, Ohio 45439
(800) 999-1007

Dynamic Focus Photography offers studio and location photography in black-and-white and color prints and slides. The studio can assist in the development of promotional materials such as brochures, catalog sheets, postcards, and business cards. Display prints and transparencies for booth exhibits are also available. Contact:

Dynamic Focus Photography
1179 Tasman Drive
Sunnyvale, California 94089
(800) 299-2515

High-Tech Printing does all types of printing jobs. Contact:

High-Tech Printing
1400 Southwest First Street
Miami, Florida 33135
(800) 323-8324

Abigail W. Simons
"Bells Are Ringing" (Porcelain
Vessel, Multi-fired with
Luster and Gold Applications)
Photo: Dynamic Focus Photography
©1994

Lucas Photographics offers four-color printing services on photo-business cards, postcards, brochures, posters, greeting cards, and reply cards. Offers free samples and newsletter. Contact:

Lucas Photographics
751 Santa Fe Drive
Denver, Colorado 80204
(303) 595-8301, or fax (303) 595-4276

Source Printers sells business cards, printed labels, tags, and rubber stamps. Write to Source Printers. Brochure is $1.

Source Printers
331 East 9th Street
New York, New York 10000
(212) 473-7833

Thurston Moore Country provides full color lithography on photo-business cards, postcards, brochures, card posters, and bookmarks (offers free samples). Contact:

Thurston Moore Country, Ltd.
204 Slayton Drive
Madison, Tennessee 37115
(615) 868-7448

ADDITIONAL DISTINCTIVE CARDS

Perfect Image Graphics Company
2429 West 12th Street
Suite 1
Tempe, Arizona 85281
(800) 533-8732

Postmark USA
280 Newport Center Drive, N. 200
Newport Beach, California 92660
(800) 999-5450

Stationery House
1000 Florida Avenue
Hagerstown, Maryland 21741
(800) 638-3033

Walter Drake
Drake Building
Colorado Springs, Colorado 80940
(719) 596-3853

Future Products
P.O. Box 27263
Tempe, Arizona 85282

Direct Promotions
P.O. Box 2487
Canoga Park, California 91306

Gentile Brothers Screen Printing
116 High Street
Edinburg, Virginia 22824
(703) 984-8852

ROLODEX-TYPE CARDS

Can you send me a price list along with samples or brochures?
How long will it take to process my order?
Do you offer any special services specifically designed to benefit artisans?

QUESTIONS TO ASK:

CHAPTER 33

Arts and Crafts Guilds and Associations

*Association
with the Best
in Your Field
Helps Sell
Your Work*

PRODUCTS BUYERS WANT: arts and crafts

COSTS TO CONSIDER: annual membership dues vary per organization, starting at $25

There are many advantages to membership in an art guild or association. Prestige can be gained by belonging to certain groups, and that prestige often translates into more money for an artisan's work. Many arts and craft guilds and associations conduct yearly shows and fairs that provide both wholesale and retail opportunities for their membership. For instance, the members of the Horse Artists Association conducted their 1992 annual sale in a Spanish hacienda gallery outside McKinney, Texas. For three days, artists from Alabama, Arizona, Illinois, and Texas, demonstrated their painting or sculpting talents. Periodically, "ten-minute" quick drawings were auctioned for an apprentice-artist-program scholarship fund. Members displayed their work, which ranged from bronze horses sculpted by Dimaro, who studied with Egyptian King Faruk's court sculptor, to oil paintings by Karen Tafoya whose canvases adorn the walls of Donald Trump's Taj Mahal Casino, to Byzantine Iconography by Debra Korluka. Artwork done by the members in the Horse Artists Association is exhibited in galleries located in all fifty states and seventeen foreign countries.

Crafts organizations can also help disseminate information concerning grants, upcoming special events, and contests. They often publish newsletters or magazines providing lists of craft courses, books, and reputable suppliers of materials. Sometimes seminars are conducted pertaining to business aspects, such as how to display work at shows or how to photograph products. Numerous associations and guilds arrange group insurance policies and help members gain access to bank credit cards.

Some organizations, such as the Horse Artists Association, arrange to have the members of longest standing help the newer members. Elizabeth Scott, who specializes in fox hunting paintings, says, "You know in the old school—artists always were apprenticed." She encourages younger artists to learn all they can from their predecessors.

SPECIAL FEATURES: Associations offer marketing collaboration that encourages members to contribute. Through cooperative efforts, an organized group can gain entry into potentially lucrative markets normally closed to individuals. The artists also help each other sell. Sherry Henderson, a sculptor who belongs to the Horse Artists Association, always presents several members' portfolios along with her own when she visits galleries in England periodically to make presentations.

HOW TO CONTACT: Local art clubs, guilds and associations are listed in the *Yellow Pages*.

For information about a reference guide to hundreds of U.S. artists' organizations entitled *Organizing Artists: Directory of the National Association of Artists' Organizations*, contact:

The American Council for the Arts
Department 43
1 East 53rd Street
New York, New York 10022
(800) 321-4510

For descriptions of arts service organizations, a guide entitled *National Association of Artists' Organizations Directory*, write:

The National Association of Artists' Organizations

918 F Street, N.W.

Washington, D.C. 20004

An easy way to locate all types of associations is by consulting *The Encyclopedia of Associations*, which is updated every two years. Each entry lists information such as the size of membership, headquarters address, telephone number, and any publications circulated by the organization. *The Encyclopedia of Associations* is available at most libraries or through:

Gale Research Inc.

835 Penobscot Building

Detroit, Michigan 48226

(800) 877-4253 or (313) 961-2242

For a *Directory of Associations in Canada*, contact:

Micro Media, Ltd.

158 Pearl Street

Toronto, Ontario M5H 113

Canada

QUESTIONS TO ASK:

What are the requirements for membership?

When would full membership be obtained?

Do you have any literature about your organization to send me?

What are the benefits of membership?

K.L. Tafoya
"A Bit of Shade" (Oil on Linen)

Visual Artist Hotline

*Help
for Artists
over
an Information
Hotline*

PRODUCT BUYERS WANT:	visual arts (painting, sculpture, drawing, crafts, photography, mixed media)
COSTS TO CONSIDER:	free

Since its founding in October 1990, the Visual Artist Hotline (800-232-2789) has processed over ten thousand calls from artists located in all fifty states, the District of Columbia, Puerto Rico, and the Virgin Islands. This toll-free service, operated by the American Council for the Arts staff, offers information on numerous topics of interest to all fine artists who are involved in any of the visual arts or in film/video.

Doug Oxenhorn, manager of the Hotline, says, "We really get asked about a wide range of things. What we can give specific information on is limited. The basic idea of the hotline is to give information referral." Hotline personnel tell callers about the names and addresses of organizations so the artists themselves can then pursue these leads. People are referred on a variety of issues such as legal information, insurance information, and artists' communities, like Yaddo, where they can go away to do work.

"The most commonly requested information is on funding," admits Oxenhorn. "Not surprisingly, people want to know about grants and where they can apply." When asked about funding, Oxenhorn, who is the author of

Money for Visual Artists, replies, "We give pretty detailed information. We try to tell them what the application and eligibility requirements are. We don't have any funding ourselves to give out."

Artists are encouraged to call, but they should keep in mind that the Hotline is primarily operated as a referral service. Details about a wide variety of programs and services available, such as the following, are provided:

■ *Public Art.* Information is given about publications that list public art programs throughout the entire country. Especially popular are the "Percent for Art" projects which direct a percentage of construction budgets for art and the "Art in Public Places" projects that position artworks in parks.

■ *International Opportunities.* Details are furnished about programs that offer both studio space and financial support to artists who will work or do research in locations outside the United States.

■ *Job Information.* The Visual Artist Hotline does not maintain job listings, but it does provide a list of newsletters and publications featuring jobs in organizations such as schools, museums, and art councils all over the nation. Information about internships and apprenticeships is also available.

■ *Artist Communities.* Referrals are made to listings of "artist colonies" throughout America which present funded and unfunded residencies to visual artists.

■ *Studio Space.* Callers are advised of programs that award free studio but not living space in Manhattan for up to one year, along with data on other studio and housing programs especially for artists.

■ *Funding and Support.* Information is given about organizations at all levels—national, regional, state and local—that directly support individual artists with cash grants or provide indirect support such as workshops and slide registries. Hotline personnel offer detailed information about grants and fellowships. This material includes the amount of money awarded, the application and selection process, who to contact, and filing deadlines. Although students are not eligible to participate in these programs, they are encouraged to call for scholarship information. Artists can contact the organizations of interest directly for guidelines and applications.

■ *Other subjects addressed are:* Group health and fine art insurance, emergency funding which helps artists in a crisis, and referrals to organizations and publications which offer legal assistance with arts-related questions such as copyright protection, contracts and estate planning.

The Visual Artist Hotline in New York City welcomes questions from all visual artists. Hotline Manager, Doug Oxenhorn, wants artists to know that "They're not alone in the struggles they're facing." The staff of the American Council for the Arts' Information Services Program will try to help by suggesting all types of publications or organizations that will assist artists in their search for information.

SPECIAL FEATURES: According to the American Council for the Arts mission statement, "The American Council for the Arts is a national organization whose purpose is to define issues and promote public policies that advance the contribution of the arts and the artist to American life." Artists do not have to be members of the American Council for the Arts to utilize their hotline services, but all artists are invited to join and thereby show their support for the organization's efforts. Membership opportunities are available at different financial levels. For example, a full member ($50), receives:

■ free subscription to *ACA UpDate*.

■ summary of the Louis Harris Poll: *Americans and the Arts VI* .

■ 10-percent discount on publications listed in the ACA Books Catalog.

■ invitations to Arts Advocacy Day, the Nancy Hanks Lecture on Arts and Public Policy, and all ACA-sponsored events.

HOW TO CONTACT:

American Council for the Arts
One East 53rd Street
New York, New York 10022

TELEPHONE CONTACT: Hours of Operation, Monday through Friday, from 2 P.M. to 5 P.M. Eastern Standard Time. If the line is busy or a call is made outside regular hours, the staff invites callers to leave a message which will be answered by mail.
Visual Artist Hotline (800) 232-2789
American Council for the Arts (212) 223-2787

QUESTIONS TO ASK:

What can you tell me about programs for artists in my state?
When is Arts Advocacy Day?
Can you give me information about travel grants funded by the National Endowment for the Arts?
Would you send me a copy of the *Hotline Services Factsheet*?
Can you send me a free *American Council for the Arts Books Catalog*?

AMERICAN COUNCIL FOR THE ARTS BOOKS

"We publish anywhere from eight to twelve new titles each year," explains Joseph Ligammari, Director of Marketing for the American Council for the Arts. "A number of them are geared to the individual artist."

Some of the books offered through the American Council for the Arts Book Catalog:

Americans and the Arts VI: Nationwide Survey of Public Opinion
Directed by Louis Harris
American Council for the Arts

Economics of Art and Culture: An American Perspective
   By James Heilbrun and Charles M. Gray
   American Council for the Arts

Race, Ethnicity, and Participation in the Arts
   Report by Paul DiMaggio and Francie Ostrower
   American Council for the Arts

Arts for Everykid: A Hand Book for Change
   By Cory Ann Alperstein and Ronnie B. Weyl
   American Council for the Arts

Arts as Education
   Edited by Merryl Ruth Goldberg and Ann Phillips
   American Council for the Arts

Money for Visual Artists: A Comprehensive Resource Guide (1993 Edition)
   Researched by Douglas Oxenhorn
   American Council for the Arts and Allworth Press

Money for International Exchange in the Arts: A Comprehensive Resource Guide
   By Jane Gullong, Noreen Tomassi, and Anna Rubin
   American Council for the Arts and Arts International

Organizing Artists: Directory of the National Association of Artists' Organizations
   National Association of Artists' Organizations

National Directory of Arts Internships 1993/94
   American Council for the Arts

Health Insurance: A Guide for Artists, Consultants, Entrepreneurs, and Other Self-Employed
   By Lenore Janecek
   American Council for the Arts

Upcoming Releases offered through the American Council for the Arts:

The Art Business Encyclopedia
   By Leonard DuBoff
   American Council for the Arts and Allworth Press
The Artist's Resource Handbook
   By Daniel Grant
   American Council for the Arts and Allworth Press

CHAPTER 35

Exhibiting in Public Buildings

Feature Your Work by Exhibiting in Public Buildings

PRODUCTS BUYERS WANT: artworks and decorative crafts

COSTS TO CONSIDER: usually free of charge

The Public Buildings Cooperative Use Act makes major public buildings all over the country accessible to the general public for commercial, educational, and recreational activities. Artists interested in showing their work to the public can often exhibit free of charge in a public government building.

The General Services Administration (GSA) is the federal government agency responsible for overseeing most public buildings.

SPECIAL FEATURE: wide exposure of work to diversified audience

Check around for public buildings as a free forum for art or crafts. For more information, write:

HOW TO CONTACT:

Federal Design Program
National Endowment for the Arts
Washington, D.C. 20506

Office of Fine Arts
General Services Administration
Washington, D.C. 20405

TELEPHONE CONTACT: For locally and regionally planned government buildings, call the Department of Public Works and ask for information from the design division, or contact the local branch of the General Services Administration under Public Buildings Service.

QUESTIONS TO ASK: How can I apply for written information about exhibiting my work in a GSA-operated building?
Will your office accept my resumé and/or slides?

Willa Frayser
"A Distant Calling" (Oil)
See related information in
Chapter 33

CHAPTER 36

Craft and Folk Art Museum

PRODUCTS BUYERS WANT: Contemporary fine crafts (art in craft media) and contemporary functional crafts (functional art and production ware). All craft media (glass, wood, clay, metal, fiber, and mixed media) are represented.

COSTS TO CONSIDER: slides, running about $25 and up

Contribute to Handmade Culture

The Craft and Folk Art Museum (CAFAM), located in Los Angeles, not far from the famous La Brea Tar Pits on Wilshire Boulevard, is a nonprofit cultural institution. The museum galleries and shop were to reopen in their new Museum Tower location in the summer of 1994. The Museum Shop showcases items created in the contemporary craft and folk art traditions, selling such items as ethnic masks, jewelry, and folk art books for both adults and children.

CAFAM realizes the impact that cultural programming has on enriching our existence. They are dedicated to the exhibition, study, preservation, and celebration of cultural expressions through the objects people use for living—their folk arts, crafts, and design.

"The library operates as primarily a marketing tool for artists to put them in touch with their potential clients. Our slide registry is for strictly what is called contemporary craft artists." Joan Benedetti, Museum Librarian, explains that the artists' work may be functional, but usually there's some sculptural or decorative aspect to it. The artwork accepted for consideration by the Craft and Folk Art Museum is "definitely in the contemporary milieu. What we're looking for is artists who are working in the contemporary craft media."

This free marketing service is operated by CAFAM for artists working in contemporary craft media in the categories of clay, enamel, fiber, glass, leather, metal, mixed media, wood, banners/kites, basketry, costume, dolls/puppets, furniture, household accessories/tableware, jewelry, masks, musical instruments, paper, and quilts. Benedetti says, "Basically, we provide a place, a large light table for potential clients to come and look at their work. We have the slides arranged in notebooks where they can be viewed very rapidly. Then we have contact information, both on computer and on a Rolodex for the easy convenience of the person looking at the slides. In addition to that we have files of other materials that an artist may want a potential client to see, lists of resumés, lists of exhibitions that their work has been in, collections that their work is in, clippings and so on. We keep it as simple as possible."

As far as who comes to look at artists' slides, Benedetti says, "We've had architects; people from the film industry—they may be looking for someone to play the part of a craftsperson or simply act as a consultant; people who are looking for teachers; people who are collectors or for whatever other reason are looking for a particular kind of work. We've also had quite a few gallery owners who are just starting up their galleries who come in here and run through our registry before they get started." All possible clients, including designers, gallery directors, and curators, are welcome to study and compare the work of artists.

"It's one of the oldest slide registries around. But we only keep work in the registry proper for five years or less. After five years, whether or not the artist gives us new slides, the old slides go into the biographical files. So they are still available, but the registry proper has only relatively new work." Benedetti adds, "Right now the registry is free both to the artist and to the potential client. The artist only has to provide us with slides and the form we give them to describe the slides."

SPECIAL FEATURES: CAFAM invites artists to submit up to twenty slides per medium or type of work enclosed in a plastic sheet (preferably "archivally correct" polyethylene plastic). Basic information about the work will be recorded. Presently, there is no charge to the artist or to the client for this service.

Professional artists or crafters should contact:

Craft and Folk Art Museum
   5800 Wilshire Boulevard
   Los Angeles, California 90036
   (213) 937-5544

HOW TO CONTACT:

Do I need to make an appointment before visiting the museum?
Could you send the application for the Artists' Slide Registry?
Approximately how many people view the museum's slide registry in one year?

QUESTIONS TO ASK:

Marilyn Todd-Daniels
"Sedona Afternoon" (Oil)
See related information in
Chapter 33

CHAPTER 37

American Craft
Association Programs

PRODUCTS BUYERS WANT: arts and crafts

COSTS TO CONSIDER: full membership: $90
student membership: $45

The American Craft Association, is a nonprofit, volunteer organization with over fourteen hundred members. The American Craft Association emerged as a new membership option offered by the American Craft Council (ACC). Their goal is to provide benefits, services, and opportunities aimed at saving both time and money for craftspeople and craft retailers. For instance, members exhibiting in ACC-operated fairs receive discounts on booth fees. They are also admitted free to ACC fairs on public days. Their spring newsletter boasts that the 5 percent booth fee discount saved member vendors $40,000 during the 1992 season.

The association offers several benefits normally difficult for craftspeople to secure on their own. As the saying goes, nothing is more valuable than your health. The American Craft Association can't offer craftspeople good health, but it can help secure the next best thing—competitively priced health insurance with a variety of program options. They also offer affordable property and casualty insurance.

Most craftspeople know how difficult it is to obtain charge cards, but

American Craft Association offers a merchant card program, which features low rates and waives the normal mandatory location requirements. Craftspeople are also automatically listed by name, address, and medium in the Association Registry.

SPECIAL FEATURE: The American Craft Association provides members with subscriptions to *The Crafts Report* and *American Craft Magazine*. They also offer a variety of educational materials, which include seminars, videotapes, audio tapes, and texts on topics requested by the membership.

HOW TO CONTACT: Craftspersons or craft retailers can contact:
American Craft Association
  Membership Services
  21 South Eltings Corner Road
  Highland, New York 12528
  (800) 724-0859, or fax (914) 883-6130

QUESTIONS TO ASK: Can you send information about the American Craft Association?
Can you send a brochure about the upcoming American Craft Council shows?
What craft legislation is the American Craft Association currently supporting in Washington?
What support do you offer craftspeople in the area of marketing?

CHAPTER 38

University Galleries

PRODUCTS BUYERS WANT: arts and crafts

COSTS TO CONSIDER: entry fees and shipping expenses, starting at about $10

Most universities, colleges, and junior colleges have art galleries where not only active students, but also all types of artisans can display their work. These schools regularly sponsor student, faculty, alumni, and guest artist shows, as well as numerous competitions. For instance, the Watkins Gallery at American University in Washington, D.C., periodically hosts specially curated exhibitions of works by nationally recognized artists. They also preside over alumni exhibitions, shows of Washington-area artists, shows of student work, and selected special exhibitions from their collection. In Dallas, the Gallery under the rotunda in Hughes-Trigg Student Center at Southern Methodist University, hosts several exhibitions every year. "Art in the Metroplex" is held at Texas Christian University's Moudy Building Exhibition Hall in Fort Worth every September.

David Conn, chairman of the Art Department at T.C.U., said over five hundred people attended their "Art in the Metroplex '92" show. This was the tenth annual presentation of the Dallas/Fort Worth region's fall juried art exhibition. Two hundred artists applied for admission; thirty were chosen for participation.

Prizes were awarded by Mr. and Mrs. Robert M. Bass, the Clardy Manufacturing Award, and the Fifth Avenue Foundation Award.

SPECIAL FEATURES: Galleries located in universities offer thousands of people the opportunity to view artisans' work. These exhibitions nurture a budding art market. The schools also offer seminars, conferences, and symposiums to help artists better understand the art market. For example, in 1993, the University of North Texas presented a valuable symposium titled "The Artist, the Dealer, the Critic, the Curator, and the Collector" (understanding the art world in terms of its interdependent careers).

HOW TO CONTACT:

Kim Rainey
San Francisco Art Institute
"King of Texas"
Binney and Smith, Inc.
University Student Grant Program

For information about the Art in the Metroplex competition, write:
Templeton Art Center
P.O. Box 9074
Fort Worth, Texas 76147

For a mailing list of seven hundred college and university art departments, contact:
Visual Studies
49 Rivoli Street
San Francisco, California 94117
(415) 664-4699

For a mailing list of over two thousand college and university galleries that exhibit work by emerging artists, contact:
ArtNetwork
13284 Rices Crossing Road
P.O. Box 369
Renaissance, California 95962-0369
(800) 383-0677 or fax (916) 692-1370

For information regarding the Liquitex Excellence in Art University Awards Program sponsored by Binney and Smith (organized to recognize outstanding undergraduate and graduate fine-arts students who have demonstrated accomplishments in the painting discipline), contact:

Binney and Smith, Inc.
    c/o Liquitex Excellence in Art
    University Student Grant Program
    1100 Church Lane
    P.O. Box 431
    Easton, Pennsylvania 18044-0431
    (215) 253-6272, or fax (215) 250-5768

QUESTIONS TO ASK:

How much does your mailing list cost?
How often are mailing lists updated?
Can you send information about any shows open to nonstudents?
Will upcoming university shows be juried?
Is the school presenting any conferences, seminars, or symposiums in the future?

Yukio Iraha
Pacific Northwest College of Art
"Mon: Gate" (Oil on
Constructed Wood)
Binney and Smith, Inc.
University Student Grant Program

Packing Your Arts and Crafts Products

U nless artisans personally deliver each of their items, they must be concerned with the problem of packing. As business grows and sales orders increase, many customers who purchase arts and crafts will be too far away to be offered personal delivery. The objective of proper packing is to get arts and crafts to their destination in good condition. How items are packed for shipment to customers is important, because first impressions are always significant. Even the most dazzling piece of pottery is not impressive if it arrives in several hundred small pieces. There is no point in assembling a perfect order only to have it damaged in shipment because of inadequate packing.

Sarah Harvey, facility manager for Meadows Gallery in Denton, Texas, talked about an impressive entry from out-of-state which was sent to be judged for possible inclusion in the gallery's annual Materials: Hard and Soft Show. The large sculpture arrived packed within two boxes that had been taped together. Unfortunately, as a result of the sculptor's slipshod packing method, the piece broke where the boxes were joined. Harvey promptly called the artist to tell him the bad news and to help him initiate a claim with the carrier. She was disappointed that, instead of being interested in how to pack his art properly in the future, all he did was angrily accuse the shipper of being careless, placing all the blame on the shipper for the broken piece.

Breakables do not present the only packing problem. Many art items require special attention to prevent their being squashed, scratched, wrinkled, or otherwise damaged in transit. Proper packing protects artwork from the rough treatment cartons may get from careless handlers or by the delivery methods used during the shipping process. In addition, the product must also be protected from the outside elements.

An artisan should never believe that the supplies and materials needed to ensure proper deliver are too costly. After all, precautions must be taken to guarantee proper packing, and this process requires extra planning, space, time, and effort. The artisan must balance the inconvenience and money spent for packing safeguards against replacing and repairing broken products, additional round-trip shipping expenses for repairs, and the costs of repairing or replacing damaged goods. Other factors that must be seriously considered are ruining the relations with the delivery service when too many claims are filed, and loss of the artist's reputation and relationship with important accounts. As the artist who wanted the one-time opportunity to enter his work in an important exhibition discovered, sometimes there is only one chance. Don't blow it!

Normally, the customer bears the costs of packing in the form of add-on costs to the price paid for the product. The fact remains that adequate shipping protection is for the user's benefit. Therefore, all costs involved inevitably should be passed on to the user as the final consumer. Depending on the business's accounting method, some artisans add a percentage of cost to the total sales price in order to compensate for packing and handling. Others simply add a flat rate to each order. Many retailers prefer to have packing and handling costs included in the price of each piece, as this method simplifies calculation of a retail selling price. Some craftspeople are reluctant to add legitimate packing costs because they are afraid that buyers might think prices are being arbitrarily raised by extra nonexistent packing expenses. However, all costs incurred in the process of creating, producing, and selling should be calculated and included in the final sales price. To do otherwise means taking a loss that could inevitably lead to lower profits.

When shipping relatively few large or expensive one-of-a-kind pieces, the packing problems are different from those involving transport of multiple production items. Each piece may require its own individually designed container which, in the case of large fragile items, should be a sturdy wooden crate. A crate can literally be built around the piece if necessary. Remember, the basic principle in packing for shipping is to protect the art from exterior and interior jostling. The artwork should be insulated in the center of the shipping container with filler material to hold the piece sturdy and keep it safe from impact.

As products are packed, generously fill in all the spaces left inside the container so that the piece or pieces in the box do not shift out of place. Stuff firmly, but don't overfill the carton so that the box bulges. Depending on what is being shipped, crumpled newspaper, plastic bubble wrap, tissue paper, white plastic foam sheeting or foam rubber will make excellent packing material. The cartons should then be sealed with strong self-adhesive packing tape, preferably reinforced. Wrapping paper cannot be secured with only transparent or masking tape. Instead, use cord or strapping/metal tape for strength when shipping by mail. Generally, the heavier the merchandise, the stronger the tape should be. Be sure to firmly secure the carton with tape.

Old crumpled newspapers are inexpensive, yet readily available, stuffing material that is quite effective for many jobs. But newsprint rubs off on whatever it touches, so only use crumpled newspapers for insulation, not for wrapping artwork that could be ruined by ink. Shredded paper, such as computer paper can also be used as an inexpensive packing material. However, shredded paper is also dusty, dirty, and compresses easily, so a package that was well-packed before shipment might in fact settle so much during transport that it leaves the product inadequately protected halfway through the trip.

One of the most popular packing materials is bubble wrap, which comes with both large and small bubbles. It is not inexpensive, but can be continuously reused as long as the bubbles remain intact. Another useful material, tissue paper, is relatively inexpensive and can be effective for an inner wrapping that is cosmetic as well as protective. White plastic foam sheeting is also another substance that is both effective and reusable. Other materials such as foam rubber can be cut to hold specific pieces. However, the high cost will probably limit its use to more expensive works of art.

Sprayed foam insulation is effective, but initial start-up costs can be prohibitive. Lots of fragile, bulky items need to be shipped to justify the initial expense.

Even old scraps of carpet can serve packing needs well, along with remnants of material and cloth and paper towels. Sometimes imaginative creations call for creative packing solutions, so try to be on the lookout constantly for new approaches.

Some craftspeople have successfully used fresh-popped popcorn for insulation, but it is not as viable an option as some might think. During transit, popcorn gets crushed to about 25 percent of its original volume, especially when protecting heavy items. This dramatic decrease in protection could cause damage during shipping, not to mention the little crumbs that end up all over everything. Popcorn also brings with it the possible problem of insects. The Popcorn Institute issued the opinion that popcorn should not be used for packing. It cite- Food and Drug Administration rules that require food, even when used for nonfood purposes, remain fit for human consumption.

Biodegradable cornstarch-based peanuts are now being sold. Eco-Foam™ peanuts dissolve in water, and can be used with any ceiling-hanging dispenser, greatly facilitating the speed and simplicity of packing. These noodle-shaped peanuts cost about twice as much as the polystyrene version, but the beneficial ecological impact is tremendous because Eco-Foam™ leaves no toxic residue when it dissolves.

For most production work, corrugated cardboard cartons are satisfactory. These boxes are available in several degrees of thickness, depending on the nature of the products to be shipped. Used boxes are one option worth considering because they are often free. Cartons may be salvaged from neighborhood supermarkets or liquor stores initially. The problem is that boxes can be hard to get in the size and quantity needed on demand. They also may project an unfavorable image. As business grows, custom cartons will need to be special ordered from professional box companies. If possible, plan to use just one single-size carton for all products shipped, because that way is definitely less expensive.

Regular-size shipping boxes are good, not too expensive, and available from paper and packaging companies. They come in a number of useful sizes with a PSI (pounds per square inch) rating of 220 pounds, which refers to the grade of cardboard rated. "T" boxes have the much stronger PSI rating of 275 pounds,

Catharine F. Kirk
Carnegie Mellon University
"The Renunciation" (Acrylic,
Charcoal on Linen)
Binney and Smith, Inc.
University Student Grant Program

thus are able to withstand more stress during the rigorous shipping process. They are generally worth the extra cost, especially for large-size artwork. It is important to remember that the strength of cardboard decreases with any increase in the size of the box. Larger boxes will have others piled high on top of them, so they need to be stronger.

One of Associated Bag Company's customers reported that its costly merchandise was getting damaged when shipped in standard corrugated boxes. The company spokesman suggested that the 275-pound test boxes be used instead. A very satisfied customer reported back, "The added strength of these sturdy boxes proved to be exactly what the customer needed, protecting both his products and his peace of mind."

Be sure to mark any special shipping instructions clearly on the outside of each carton. Glass and other fragile articles should have the standard wine glass symbol stenciled on each side of the box. Bright-colored fragile and rush stickers can be ordered from several suppliers of packing products. Clearly write the address directly on the carton with a waterproof marker or affix a gummed label with the address typed. Mark the return address prominently on the outside of the carton. It is not a bad idea to enclose the name, address, and telephone number of the company or artisan inside the box, too. Packing list envelopes can be imprinted with logo and company name using camera-ready artwork to help artisans get their advertising message out.

Shippers such as United Parcel Service (UPS) should be consulted in advance regarding any special instructions or requirements they may require. For instance, UPS requires that all seams and edges of each box be taped. Transparent tape must cover the label to prevent accidental erasure of the address. For more information on UPS shipping requirements, contact the nearest local United Parcel Service office.

The golden rule of packing is to always think about the safe arrival of the product at its intended destination. Consider the kind of accidents that can happen to unprotected items during transit, and then pack to withstand these potential abuses. Don't spend valuable time worrying about products' safe arrival. Instead, spend that time pursuing profitable artistic activities.

HOW TO FIND PACKING MATERIALS

To find a local box supplier, look under Paper Supplies or Packing in the *Yellow Pages*. Or, to acquire more information about various types of packing materials, contact the following mail order firms:

Associated Bag Company supplies boxes and packing materials to ship and store anything from fragile products to heavy, bulky items such as automotive parts. One of the company's mottos is, "If you're having trouble finding a solution to your weighty shipping problems, we're always ready with some strong advice." For bags (bubble, burlap, cloth, foam, write-on, zipper), corrugated shipping boxes, Eco-Foam™, imprinted packing list envelopes, mailing envelopes, mailing tubes, peanuts, tape, write:

Associated Bag Company
400 West Boden Street
Milwaukee, Wisconsin 53207-7120
(800) 926-6100

OCS Shipping Service provides domestic and international shipping. Write or call for free estimates on all crating needs. Contact:

OCS Shipping Service
36 White Street
New York, New York 10013
(212) 226-1052, or fax (212) 431-3903

Packaging Un-Limited manufactures its own boxes so they are ready to be shipped immediately. The company can supply self-locking mailer boxes, optical boxes, tote boxes, bin boxes, record storage boxes, coin boxes, triangular-shape boxes, hat boxes, jewelry boxes, videotape mailer boxes, and videotape storage boxes. Both recycled padded self-sealing mailers and recycled bubble cushioned self-sealing mailers can be provided along with bubble wrap rolls and peel-and-stick fliptop bubble bags plus packing list envelopes, corner protectors, tissue paper, tape, and dispensers. Contact:

Packaging Un-Limited Incorporated
1121 West Kentucky Street
Louisville, Kentucky 40210
(800) 585-4955
Inside Kentucky: (502) 584-4331, or fax (502) 585-4955

Springfield Corrugated Box Company will provide a free catalog of corrugated boxes, made-to-order boxes, moving boxes along with tape, packing supplies, Bubble-Pak, colored and white, waxed tissue, or shredded newspaper. Contact:

Springfield Corrugated Box Company, Inc.
P.O. Box 714
74 Moylan Lane
Agawam, Massachusetts 01001
(800) 437-8453 or (413) 789-2268, or fax (413) 789-2313

Strongbox provides superior shock absorption through the use of two layers of convoluted foam and one layer of Perf-Pack foam. The Perf-Pack layer allows you to custom-fit Stongbox to the exact dimensions of a frame. Contact:

Guildhall, Inc.
2535 Weisenberger Street
Fort Worth, Texas 76107
(800) 356-8100

Mary Bell
Montclair State College
"Dryland/Wetland" (Oil on
Linen)
Binney and Smith, Inc.
University Student Grant Program

CHAPTER 39

Selling to Europe

Don't Pass up the Chance to Show Europe Your Talent

PRODUCTS BUYERS WANT: arts and crafts

COSTS TO CONSIDER: Export license fees, duties, and shipping. Expect to start off paying $100 or so.

E xceptional opportunities exist for astute artisans overseas, especially since Europeans have always cherished fine craftsmanship. If artisans decide that their products have foreign sales potential, then possible profit from sales should be weighed against the complications of exporting. Since any exporting mistakes can be costly, clarify concerns by asking who, what, where, when, why, and how questions that need to be answered before doing business. For example: Whom do we deal with at your company? What documents are necessary? When should we begin shipping? Where is the best place for products to arrive? Why does the product have to be shipped that way? How do we proceed once a deal is made?

When an inquiry is received that is not in English, an interpreter or a local college's foreign language department may be contacted for an exact translation. Incidentally, it is not diplomatic to ask the sender to dispatch future correspondence in English. Receipt of an inquiry should be acknowledged immediately. Any questions can be faxed or telexed in the language of the sender. AT&T now offers an international FAXLine service to several countries in

Europe. A two-page fax message that should take about one minute to transmit costs $1.71 if sent to France during a business day.

Make certain that all aspects of the customer's inquiry, such as what is being ordered, amounts, terms, and delivery schedule, are fully understood. Review the credit and reputation of the inquirer with an international banker or a private company that performs international business checks. Then decide what credit terms are acceptable. Once an order is received, verify the agreed-upon information, then let the senders know that their order has been accepted and will be filled quickly. The wording on any letter of credit must be examined. Any changes deemed necessary should be requested and should take effect immediately. Notify the customer when the order is shipped, including both the name of the carrier and bill of lading number.

Instead of trying to make all the connections themselves, some crafters may decide to work through export sales representatives. Others work through show promoters such as The Rosen Group, creator of the Buyers Markets of American Crafts Shows. In this case, the agency manages details like taking American crafts to Europe then presenting them at craft shows. The Rosen Group also takes orders and then oversees all the shipping arrangements, including customs declaration forms. To compensate for their sales efforts, the agency receives a 15 percent commission. Every August in Frankfurt, Germany, the Rosen Group holds its main show—"Messe Frankfurt."

With the assistance now available, sending products to Europe is not much more difficult than shipping merchandise anywhere in the United States.

TIPS FOR DOING BUSINESS IN EUROPE	■ Learn as much as possible about international trade before making commitments that may not be fully understood.
	■ Make sure to deal with a reputable European company by asking for references located in the United States that can easily be verified.
	■ Listen carefully to the English being spoken so that there is no misunderstanding. Although most Europeans speak English, some speak the language better than others and there are many subtleties in meaning. It

is a good idea to follow-up immediately, confirming the important points of conversation in writing.

- ■ Fax machines are vital to effective and fast communications with Europeans.
- ■ Learn the language of European business. Find out about the international paperwork that affects shipping products.

SPECIAL FEATURE: Exporting artwork broadens an artisan's customer base while enhancing both the domestic image and the image abroad. Therefore, product life is extended.

HOW TO CONTACT:

AT&T's International FAXLine has an "establishment fee" of $10. Customers are obligated to use $5 minimum monthly usage.

Call AT&T at (800) 222-0400.

For information about doing business in Europe through The Rosen Group, contact:

The Rosen Group
3000 Chestnut Avenue
Suite 300
Baltimore, Maryland 21211
(410) 889-2933

The Crafts Report, a monthly publication, tells about upcoming shows to be held in Europe, listing foreign events under Wholesale Show Dates. For subscription information, contact:

The Crafts Report
P.O. Box 1992
Wilmington, Delaware 19899-9962
(800) 777-7098, or fax (302) 656-4894

RESOURCES: The World Crafts Council Directory/Europe provides information about government agencies, activities (concerning crafts, galleries, trade fairs, craft events and other areas) in several European countries. Write:

World Crafts Council
P.O. Box 2045
DK 1012
Copenhagen K, Denmark

Sourcebooks for artists and craftspeople with details about exhibiting opportunities in Europe are *Across Europe: The Artist's Personal Guide to Opportunity* and *Action and Making Connections: The Craftsperson's Guide to Europe*. Ordering details are available from:

AN Publications
Freepost, Box 23
Sunderland SR1 1BR
England

For information about contacting galleries, museums, and alternative spaces, a series of books is available through these Art Guide publications:

Amsterdam Art Guide, edited by Christian Reinwald
Berlin Art Guide, edited by Irene Blumenfield
Glasgow Art Guide, edited by Alice Bain
London Art and Artists' Guide, edited by Heather Waddell
Madrid Arts Guide, edited by Claudia Oliveira Cezar
Paris Art Guide, edited by Fiona Dunlop

Available from:
Art Guide Publications
Talman Company, Inc.
150 Fifth Avenue
New York, New York 10011

For information on how to obtain Guide to Financing Exports, write:

U.S. and Foreign Commercial Service
 International Trade Administration
 Room 1617
 U.S. Department of Commerce
 Washington, D.C. 20230

A thirty-five-minute videotape, *Basics of Exporting*, is available through the Small Business Administration. Call (800) U-ASK-SBA.

 The U.S. government has published a guide to federal international trade programs offered by ten agencies, including the Small Business Administration. Publication #045-000-00250-1, which costs $4, contains program overviews and fifty pages of contact names and addresses, speakers on special topics, and a bibliography of relevant agency publications, including the following:

 Basic Guide to Exporting #003-009-00315-6
 European Trade Fairs: A Guide for American Exporters
 Export Trading Company Guidebook #003-009-00523-0
 Foreign Business Practices
 Monthly Exports and Imports—Report #925
 Partners in Export Trade #003-009-00512-4

To order these publications, contact:

Superintendent of Documents
 U.S. Government Printing Office
 Washington, D.C. 20402
 (202) 783-3238

For specific questions regarding export write:

United States Customs Service
 1301 Constitution Avenue
 Washington, D.C. 20229

GOVERNMENT SOURCES OF INFORMATION ABOUT EXPORTING:

QUESTIONS TO ASK: How long will it take to receive the materials I have ordered?

Do you have any new books, brochures, or materials on this subject coming out?

BOOKS: *Building an Import/Export Business*
Kenneth D. Weiss
John Wiley and Sons: New York
Explains how to cope with shipping, insurance, customers, and getting paid for international transactions.

Export Profits: A Guide for Small Businesses
Jack S. Wolf
Upstart Publishing Company, Inc.
Dover, New Hampshire
(800) 235-8866 or (603) 749-5071
This book is by an international trade consultant who runs an innovative program at the University of Massachusetts that has helped hundreds of businesses enter foreign markets.

Import/Export: A Guide to Growth, Profits, and Market Share
Prentice Hall
Englewood Cliffs, New Jersey
This comprehensive guide for small to medium-size companies addresses distributing, pricing, financing, licensing, shipping, and government restrictions.

Profitable Exporting: A Complete Guide to Marketing Your Products Abroad
John S. Gordon and J. R. Arnold
John Wiley and Sons: New York

CHAPTER 40

Church Bazaars, Sales, and Events

PRODUCTS BUYERS WANT: arts and crafts

COSTS TO CONSIDER: Cost of booth rental. This could run in the neighborhood of $25 or more.

Benefit from Bazaars!

Buyers who shop church and charity bazaars appreciate handcrafted work. These shoppers want to purchase one-of-a-kind items at reasonable prices. If the bazaar is always held annually, then the chances of selling craft items greatly improve. The weekend before the Thanksgiving holiday is a popular time for selling at arts and crafts events held in churches. For example, one week preceding Thanksgiving, an annual bazaar was conducted at Eastminster Presbyterian Church in Dallas and, simultaneously, a craft fair was held at Mary Immaculate Church in nearby Farmers Branch. The proximity of these events made traveling to both sales quite easy for holiday shoppers.

To increase the odds for making a profit at bazaars, it is vital that craftspeople select settings that are best-suited for showcasing their products. It is wise for artisans to visit the spots where they wish to sell their products the year before they want to enter this potentially profitable market, in order to familiarize themselves with this type of selling environment. Bear in mind that bazaars also furnish a great place to conduct market research where new items

Nina Koepcke
"Dish Ran Away with the Spoon"
(Found Objects Fired into
Handbuilt Clay with Glaze)
See related information in
Chapter 32
Photo: Dynamic Focus Photography
©1994

can be tried, prices tested, and artistic designs watched to see which sell best. After selecting a site, to achieve the most success at bazaars artisans should:

- Try to dress like the shoppers who will attend. If possible, wear items that you sell, such as T-shirts, jewelry, or hats.

- Determine in advance what equipment, such as tables and chairs, will be furnished.

- Find out which facilities, like bathrooms or drinking fountains, are available to participants.

- Ask what percentage of the exhibitor's receipts are required to be donated to the sponsoring organization. Normally, a portion of the requested amount goes toward advertising and rental costs.

Sometimes crafters are asked to submit a sample or slides of their work to a screening committee. These jurors will determine whether or not crafters' items will fit the needs of bazaar planners before an invitation is extended to exhibit.

SPECIAL FEATURE: Churches and synagogues have demonstrated an interest in art for many years. Places of worship often contain stained glass, tapestries, murals, sculpture, and other artistic accessories which embellish their buildings, so most tend to be sensitive to artisans' endeavors. Bazaars held in these places furnish excellent exposure, especially for beginning craftspeople. In fact, some participants find that these annual bazaars provide more than sufficient outlets for their products.

HOW TO CONTACT: Chambers of Commerce produce calendars of events that often include information about local bazaars.

A membership organization called Catholic Art Society produces temporary art shows. They also maintain a slide registry. For additional information, write:

Catholic Art Society
    212 East 47th Street
    New York, New York 10017
    (212) 752-3785

Artists can also contact local churches, schools, and charitable institutions listed in the telephone yellow pages. Often, shows are conducted in such varied places as parish houses, auditoriums, or Sunday-school rooms.

QUESTIONS TO ASK:

How much will the booth space cost?
What are the opening and closing hours?
Is electricity furnished?
How many shoppers usually attend this event?
What are the dimensions of the booths?
Is the booth backed by a wall or open on all sides?
How will the bazaar be publicized?

Sherry Henderson
"Ghost Horse"
See related information in
Chapter 33
Photo: Sherry Henderson

CHAPTER 41

U.S. Department of Interior: Indian Arts and Crafts Board

A Free Listing for Native Americans in the Source Directory

PRODUCTS BUYERS WANT: Native American arts and crafts

COSTS TO CONSIDER: none

"There is great public demand for Native American crafts at present," according to the *Source Directory* printed by the U.S. Department of Interior. They want to alert buyers to products made by Indian, Eskimo, and Aleut owned-and-operated arts and crafts businesses. Crafts displayed for sale through the *Source Directory* include a wide variety of original products. Handcrafted items range from Eskimo wood masks supplied by the Alaska Native Arts and Crafts Association in Anchorage to Zuni, Navajo, Chippewa, and Hopi silverwork from the La Ray Turquoise Company located in Cody, Wyoming. Pictures of all types of other impressive creations such as bolo ties, shawls, Nez Perce baskets, hand-carved model canoes, patchwork dolls, and porcupine quill boxes fill the directory's pages.

Included in the *Source Directory* are: 1) artist and craftsmen cooperatives, 2) tribal arts and crafts enterprises, 3) businesses privately owned and operated by Native American designers/craftsmen and artists, and 4) businesses privately owned and operated by Native American merchants who retail and/or wholesale authentic Native American arts and crafts.

Most of the sources listed maintain retail shops that welcome visitors. Several of the businesses offer mail-order services. Nonprofit organizations such as the North American Indian Association of Detroit also work directly with Native American groups to develop products and markets.

SPECIAL FEATURE: The *Source Directory* is a not an order catalog, so detailed information about products and prices must be obtained directly from each listing.

HOW TO CONTACT: For information concerning contemporary Indian, Eskimo, and Aleut arts and crafts, contact:

Indian Arts and Crafts Board
Mail Stop 4004-MIB
1849 C Street, N.W.
U.S. Department of the Interior
Washington, D.C. 20240
(202) 208-3773

QUESTIONS TO ASK: Can you send me any literature about the *Source Directory*?
What factors qualify me for participation in this program?

CHAPTER 42

Slide Registries

*Pictures
Reveal
Your Talents
to Thousands*

....

PRODUCTS BUYERS WANT: arts and crafts

....

COSTS TO CONSIDER: slides: $25 and up

....

Slide registries are created to bridge the gap between buyers interested in arts and crafts and sellers who want to find the right placement for their work. Professional artists benefit from inclusion because many museum curators, government agencies, architects, interior designers, sales representatives, and dealers find desirable artwork by consulting slide registries. Registries enable artists to have their work viewed outside their immediate location. Interested parties are then advised on how to reach the artist.

Well-photographed slides are vital to acceptance by slide registries. Artisans who are unable to photograph their work professionally should find an expert photographer who will portray artistic items to the best advantage. Usually this involves finding a specialist in product photography.

Only the most appealing artwork should be selected for submission. As far as other photographic considerations, Brian Ramey of Dynamic Focus Photo-graphy in Sunnyvale, California, advises, "Lighting and backgrounds should bring out the most important design elements of the objects being photographed."

Often choosing a black, gray, or white background will showcase artwork most advantageously. Professional artists label each slide with name, address, the media (watercolor, oil, or other types of artwork), edition size, and the date work was completed. The top of the slide must be annotated with the word "top," as well as size, height, and width of the work. Arrange slides, then number each one so that the viewer can follow the sequence on an accompanying reference sheet. Slides should be protectively encased in plastic sleeves, which can be purchased from camera and photography stores.

Slide registries are indispensable. They are a valuable aid for artists desiring further exposure for their work.

SPECIAL FEATURE: Arts and crafts periodicals often list existing slide registries or those being organized that are applicable to the intended audience.

HOW TO CONTACT: Some city arts councils and art associations authorize slide registries for artists and craftspeople in their community. Contact city officials at these councils and associations to find out if they have established artists' slide registries or if they have plans for developing any in the future.

The Rockland Center for the Arts in Rockland City, New York, is a good example of such a resource. They invite all artists who reside in Rockland City to submit slides along with resumés for the Center's Artists' Registry." All works that are submitted will be considered for upcoming shows at Rockland Center for the Arts.

QUESTIONS TO ASK: How long will my slides be kept on file?
Is this slide registry juried?
How many other artists are on file that are in my artistic or geographic area?
Is a listing fee charged?
If a fee is charged, how much?

Museum of Neon Art

704 Traction

Los Angeles, California 90013

Will review and consider slides of neon art, but enclose a self-addressed stamped envelope (SASE)

New England Artists' Registry

P.O. Box 165

Housatonic, Massachusetts 01236

A computerized slide registry for New England artists.

Western New York Slide File

c/o Hallwalls Contemporary Arts Center

700 Main Street

Buffalo, New York 14202

Artists located in Buffalo and Western New York are invited to submit slides, photos, and resumés.

Selection Committee

55 Mercer Gallery

55 Mercer Street

New York, New York 10013

Seeks submissions of slides and resumés for guest artist shows; details available by SASE.

ADDITIONAL SLIDE REGISTRIES

Marilyn Todd-Daniels
"Andalusian Piaffe" (Oil)
See related information in
Chapter 33
Kelli Murphy in Sanger, Texas

Artsline

Elspeth Marrison

5 Crowndale Road

London NW1 1TU

England

An information resource that lists disabled artists.

INTERNATIONAL SLIDE REGISTRIES

South East Arts

Crafts Officer

10 Mount Ephraim

Tunbridge Wells

Kent TN4 8AS

England

A directory of professional craftspeople and artists living in Kent, East Sussex, and Surrey.

Gallerie Publications

2901 Panorama Drive, North

Vancouver, British Columbia, Canada V7G 2A4

(604) 929-8706

Contemporary women artists are invited to send information about themselves and their work.

ADA

32 Eland Road

London SW11 5JY

Presently, this database is concentrating on British women artists both living and dead, and then will later expand to include women artists from other countries.

MAILING LISTS

ArtNetwork

13284 Rices Crossing Road

P.O. Box 369

Renaissance, California 95962-0369

(800) 383-0677, or fax (916) 692-1370

For a mailing list of 125 art organization slide registries where artists' work is seen by serious collectors, and for a mailing list of 125 Art Council Slide Registries which provide an important art source for collectors and architects.

Art Calendar

P.O. Box 872

Great Falls, Virginia 22066

(703) 759-3485

A monthly newsletter that lists slide registries offering professional opportunities for visual artists.

Marilyn Todd-Daniels
"Going to Market" (Oil)
See related information in
Chapter 33

Carol Ostheller of Alphabet Kids
Heidi Dress
Photo: Carol Ostheller

43

Handmade in America Shows

....

PRODUCTS BUYERS WANT: arts and crafts handmade in America

....

COSTS TO CONSIDER: Cost of mall space starts at $350 per show.

....

Travel from Aventura Mall in Florida to Walt Whitman Mall in New York with lucrative stops along the way at over twenty malls such as Lynnhaven Mall in Virginia, Ocean County Mall in New Jersey, and Franklin Mills in Pennsylvania. Craftspersons who elect to join the Handmade in America Show will follow an itinerary that offers the opportunity for display of U.S. merchandise at shopping malls located in several states along the eastern seaboard. Last year's exhibitors reported gross sales of over $1 million, which came to almost $2,500 per exhibitor per show.

Membership entitles professional artisans to participate in any of the mall shows as long as space and craft category are still available. Exhibitors are required to actively demonstrate their skills at the malls in front of shoppers. Interested artisans should fill out their membership application, then send it, along with three slides or photographs of their work and one picture of how their merchandise was displayed during a previous show. Special discounts for hotel/motel accommodations and restaurants are also offered.

If being a demonstrating artist or craftsperson as part of a show tour sounds like it would be advantageous for business, then the Handmade in America

Show organizers want to receive an application. Each crafter's work is guaranteed to be viewed by thousands of interested shoppers who want to buy American goods.

SPECIAL FEATURES: The Handmade in America Show organizers provide an informative newsletter to all members. Support materials such as aprons for exhibitors to wear, signs, and show flyers are made available at each mall.

HOW TO CONTACT: For membership information:
Handmade In America Shows
251 Creekside Drive
Saint Augustine, Florida 32086
(904) 797-2600

QUESTIONS TO ASK: What is the rent on the different size spaces?
How many craftspeople participate in shows?
Can you send me your *Show Calendar* and *Mall Street Journal*?

CHAPTER 44

Swap Meets

*Put Your
Arts and Crafts
to Work
Every Weekend
at Swap Meets*

PRODUCTS BUYERS WANT: art and crafts

COSTS TO CONSIDER: Standard space rents for approximately $250 and up for a four-week period that includes twelve selling days (Friday-Sunday).

If working on weekends to make money sounds good, then selling at swap meets is an option that fits into the busiest schedule. At many shows, vendors are required to carry entirely new merchandise. Some indoor shows feature more than seven hundred exhibitors. If a show is held indoors, then usually all the merchandise is new. Shows held outdoors often carry both new and used goods for sale.

SPECIAL FEATURES: Markets as big as several football fields (some enclosed) with thousands of shoppers every weekend offer boundless possibilities for selling to many customers, making connections, and networking.

HOW TO CONTACT: A national directory that includes swap meets, flea markets, trade days, and dealer auctions is available from:

The Great American Flea Market Directory
> P.O. Box 543
> Fenton, Missouri 63026

The 1994 Guide to Active Flea Markets and Swap Meets, and directories of active, operating, and predominantly new merchandise markets across the United States are The Merchandiser Group's Guides (*East Coast Merchandiser*, *Midwest Merchandiser*, and *West Coast Merchandiser*) and are available from:

Sumner Communications
> Grassy Plain Street
> Bethel, Connecticut 06801

For information about indoor swap meets held in Las Vegas, Nevada, and Tucson, Arizona (vendors with new merchandise), contact:

Indoor SwapMart
> 5115 North 27th Avenue
> Phoenix, Arizona 85017
> (602) 246-9600

For information about newsletters, guides and ongoing swap meets in California, contact:

Swap Meets West
> 295 N. Broadway, #147
> Santa Maria, California 93455
> (805) 928-2205

QUESTIONS TO ASK: Would you send me information regarding swap meets?
How many people attend your swap meet in one weekend?

CHAPTER 45

Special Outlets for Senior Citizens

The Best is Yet to Be

....

PRODUCTS BUYERS WANT: arts and crafts by people aged fifty-five and over

....

COSTS TO CONSIDER: Cost of long-distance telephone and samples. Figure on about $25 or more.

....

The Elder Crafters Shop in Old Town Alexandria, Virginia, beckons tourists who are visiting the eighteenth-century Gadsby's Tavern Museum across the street. Visitors can browse through the quilts, pottery, dollhouse furniture, jewelry, sweaters, and Christmas ornaments as long as they wish. A variety of functional wood items such as toys, trays, and sewing boxes also attract the shoppers' attention.

Norma Erskine, bookkeeper for the Elder Crafters Shop, says, "They won't accept anything that's not of quality." Her reference is to the selection committee that meets on the first Saturday of each month to register new elder crafters, either in person or by mail. This shop carries only work from crafters that are over fifty-five years of age. Craft items in the Elder Crafters Shop are shipped from artisans in several states, including Arizona, California, Florida, Iowa, and New Hampshire.

The work of these elder crafters often continues longtime family traditions. Items in the store range in price from one dollar for pen-and-ink cards depicting historic sites, to $950 for Amish quilts. Crafters are asked the appraised value of their work, then 40 percent is added to cover the shop's expenses.

SPECIAL FEATURES: Not only can participating crafters supplement their incomes through this program, but they can also perfect old and new skills, assist in running of the shop, and enrich their retirement years by sharing many enjoyable hours with peers.

HOW TO CONTACT: American handcrafters over the age of fifty-five contact:
Elder Crafters of Alexandria, Inc.
405 Cameron Street
Alexandria, Virginia 22314
(703) 683-4338
Open Tuesday through Saturday from 10 A.M to 4 P.M.

QUESTIONS TO ASK: What kind of samples do you accept?
Will sample(s) be returned?
How long is unsold work allowed to remain in the shop?

OTHER SHOPS FOR SENIOR CRAFTERS: Senior citizen craft shops usually work with consignment merchandise, often doing a large volume of business. They are normally staffed by volunteer help. Often these type of craft shops carry a wider variety of craft work than do craft galleries or any single retail outlet. Those interested should research pricing carefully, paying close attention to what the market will pay for their type of work.

American handcrafters over the age of fifty-five should check with local senior-citizen organizations or their local Chamber of Commerce office to locate shops.

Shops that have welcomed elder crafters include RSVP Craft House (San Francisco, California), Golden Eagle Elder Craftsmen Shop (Wilmington,

Delaware), Senior Citizen Handicraft Shop (Kansas City, Kansas), Elder Craftsmen (Chicago, Illinois), Project Homespun (Boston, Massachusetts), Senior Citizen Craft Shop (Independence, Missouri), Master Crafters (Manhasset, New York), Elder Craftsmen Shop (New York, New York), Elder Craftsmen (Philadelphia, Pennsylvania), Northwest Senior Craftsmen (Seattle, Washington), and The Golden Ladder (Englewood, New Jersey).

For information about a book listing more than two hundred shops across the country interested in selling work of elder craftspeople over age sixty, write:

The Elder Craftsmen
135 East 65th Street
New York, New York 10021

Lynne Rutherford
Pin (Vintage Watch Parts)
See related information in
Chapter 17
Photo: Lynne Rutherford

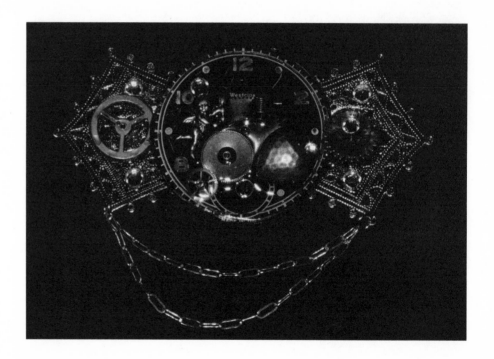

CHAPTER 46

Kiosks and Pushcarts

PRODUCTS BUYERS WANT: arts and crafts

COSTS TO CONSIDER: Kiosk rental rates range from $200 to $500 a week during the off-season; from $300 to more than $1,000 a week during the prime holiday season. Often a percentage of the cart vendor's gross sales (usually 10 to 20 percent) are paid to the mall after sales reach predetermined levels.

Pushcart Your Way Down the Road to Financial Success

A new merchandising outlet is the specialty vendor cart, frequently called pushcarts or kiosks. These mobile merchandising display booths are available for rental at most major shopping malls. Portable retail units offer a means for fledgling retailers to test their sales skills and the market for their arts and crafts products. This market research is an especially valuable process if crafters' products are not readily available in stores and do not compete with merchandise sold by other mall merchants.

Kiosks bring new items to shopping centers while offering a means for all types of retailers to test market their product's sales potential. Vendor carts also appeal to small business owners because they can be rented for short time periods. Over the years, pushcarts have become valued for providing mall management with extra dollars from additional rents.

Gail Bird, author of *Cart Your Way to Success—A Peddler's Play in Three Acts*, was called in for consultation by the developers of the pushcart program at West End Market in Dallas. "I was called in when they were in the planning stages," Bird said. "I was asked how to put together a pushcart program that was effective and what from the vendor's point of view makes it successful, since if the vendor is successful, then the management is successful."

Bird also offers lectures to people who are interested in pursuing the pushcart business. She says, "Mainly, it's on how to negotiate a lease in your favor, how to position yourself, what products work and don't work, what revenue you can expect (not what they expect), how many hours it really is (eighty a week), and what kind of help you can get since these are transient jobs."

Bird says that she made a good living operating a pushcart. "They are a great entry into retail marketing if you don't have a lot of money and this is what you think you want to do. You should run and manage and own a pushcart, because you only need $5,000. You don't need $150,000, $350,000, $500,000 to see if you want to be a retailer."

ADVANTAGES TO KIOSK OR PUSHCART SELLING

- Since there is no need to invest in the costs involved with operating a full-fledged store, there is low overhead with minimal investment.

- Goods are normally shown in a high-visibility location—right in the middle of mall traffic.

- Kiosk rental can be for conveniently short periods of time, such as weekends when there are no craft fairs scheduled.

- Cart programs bring a better selection of merchandise to a mall, which helps all the retailers by attracting a more diverse audience.

- Mall pushcarts and kiosks can be used for test-marketing new products.

- Renting a cart or kiosk is an excellent way to establish a good reputation with mall management. Theresa Little from Melvin Simon and Associates says, "Sunshine Artists always provide a beautiful setup using antique furniture as a backdrop for their arts and crafts. They will always be invited to return to Golden Triangle Mall (Denton, Texas). They know what we expect from the merchandising end. You'd better be supplied with enough merchandise to last all of the holiday season, because nothing looks worse than an empty booth toward the end of the season."

■ Hours that the shopping mall requires the pushcart to be operated, usually from 10:00 A.M. until 9:00 P.M., can be challenging for working crafters to maintain. Long hours are especially arduous when the craftsperson is simultaneously trying to make more crafts to sell. ■ The limited space available on a kiosk for display of merchandise can be quite restrictive. ■ Mall management usually wants to see a professional display of the craftsperson's work. This will involve using well-designed pieces and props. **SPECIAL FEATURES:** Colorful display carts can be works of art in themselves. Many times portable retail units are constructed to look like old-fashioned street vendors' carts. These kiosks offer a festive presentation for arts and crafts, thus providing maximum exposure to mall traffic, which prompts impulse buying from customers.	**DRAWBACKS TO KIOSK OR PUSHCART SELLING**
Check with local mall managers about cart rental programs. Most will have information packets available for artists and crafters interested in vendor cart or kiosk rentals.	**HOW TO CONTACT:**

QUESTIONS TO ASK: How much does it cost to rent a kiosk?

What is the shortest amount of time I can rent a pushcart?

Are there special requirements for the cart's decor?

What area of the mall will my kiosk occupy?

Can you advise me on how to obtain insurance?

ADDITIONAL READING   *Cart Your Way to Success—A Peddler's Play in Three Acts*, by Gail Bird ($19.95 plus $2 shipping and handling). A guide for artisans who would like to get into crafts merchandising with pushcarts in shopping malls. Contact:

Birdhouse Enterprises

110 Jennings Avenue

Patchogue, New York 11772

(516) 654-1044

Golden Triangle Mall Administrator

Theresa Little, office administrator for Melvin Simon and Associates (who manage Golden Triangle Mall in Denton, Texas) says that the key to successful kiosk selling at malls is meeting customer demand by producing items, in sufficient quantity, that customers want to buy. This is especially true during the holiday season, when "rates change drastically for November and December." It is during this time that malls really "need products people are looking for," Little says. "You had better be supplied with enough merchandise to last all season, because nothing looks worse than an empty booth toward the end of a season." It is important that the quantity of merchandise available be sufficient to meet the demand during the entire sales period. She says that vendors must be prepared for the "push" at the end of the holiday season.

Golden Triangle Mall offers professional wooden carts for seasonal rental. The dimensions are 36"x84" with a five-inch ledge on all four sides. There are four wooden adjustable shelves along with one large and one small compartment with locks. The wood is three-quarter-inch birch veneered plywood with a fire-resistant canvas canopy in tan, brown, and white stripes. A plastic signage holder is attached to the canopy. The lighting is two UL-approved fluorescent bulbs.

Cart-rental charges are based on the length of sales period, merchandise season, expected sales volumes, location in mall, and product type. Applications for the winter holiday season are due in June. A general price range for cart rental for the entire Christmas season starts at $3,300. Little points out that "cost is negotiated on an individual basis." All temporary tenants must provide a certificate of insurance that verifies that an effective policy is in effect with comprehensive liability coverage of $1 million.

In addition to the wooden carts with canvas tops, Golden Triangle Mall offers four ten-foot-by-ten-foot booths and one eight-foot-by-eight-foot booth for rental. Booth and cart displays are required to be professionally designed. No magic markers or stencil signs such as "Employee Wanted" are allowed.

Little says, "We are always looking for arts and crafts because they sell so well in this particular area." The arts and crafts must not be sold through any of the mall's other stores. The "tenant mix" is crucial to mall management. The quality of merchandise must be excellent. Product guarantees to customers are essential. All merchants are asked to keep their kiosks open during mall hours even if hours of operation have been extended for the holidays. The sales staff is required to maintain a neat personal appearance, which means dressing in appropriate business attire. Efficient, courteous service is expected at all times.

Sunshine Artists has sold its stained glass work at Golden Triangle for several holiday seasons. Little says these artists have an open invitation to return every year because "they know what we expect from the merchandising end. Their lovely setups with antique furniture and beautiful scarves always fit in so perfectly."

The mall management has a packet of information which helps artists and crafts workers in deciding whether cart selling at malls would be a viable option for them. Information such as shopper demographics gives a profile of mall customers; a fact sheet lists the anchor stores, tenant mix, and parking places; temporary tenant guidelines tell vendors what the rules are and what behavior will be expected from them at the mall; and a mall map shows the locations of all tenants along with sizes of their stores. A tenant leasing inquiry form is included so artisans will know what types of questions will be asked regarding their projected selling activities.

All malls have guidelines. It is important for artisans to find out if they will be able to comply with these guidelines before making even a short-term commitment. The following are some of Golden Triangle Mall's rules and regulations for temporary vendors:

- The user will man the booth/display area at all times and will remain in the assigned area to conduct business during regular mall hours.

- Lunches and breaks are not to be taken in the mall common area or in a booth/display area. Smoking is not permitted in any display area or booth structure.

- Hours of operation must coincide with the hours the Golden Triangle Mall is open.

- No carnival-type "barking" or other similar types of "hard sell" tactics or badgering of Golden Triangle Mall patrons is allowed. No radios or televisions are allowed unless they are used in merchandising a product.

- User shall be solely responsible for policing its location against theft, loss, or damage to user's property. If the user requires security, the user will be responsible for hiring and paying for security officers, subject to the mall management's approval.

- Any exhibit/booth utilizing hazardous materials such as oxygen or acetylene bottles must meet all local and state safety requirements. The mall office must approve, in advance, all such uses.

- Alterations to the physical structure of the Golden Triangle Mall are prohibited.

- Utilities, if needed, will be supplied by the center. Electrical wiring should not be visible.

- User is responsible for maintenance and clean-up of the area used.

- No pets may be brought into the mall or tied at any of the mall entrances.

- User and any employees will be required to park on the perimeter of the parking lot, as designated by the mall management. Overnight parking is not allowed.

- Under no circumstances will user be allowed to bring any material into the mall or begin operating without first having completed the proper paper-work and having supplied owner with a current certificate of insurance.

- Photos or drawings of kiosk display must be submitted for landlord approval.

CHAPTER 47

Co-op Galleries

Connect with Customers— Join a Co-op

PRODUCTS BUYERS WANT: arts and crafts

COSTS TO CONSIDER: Co-op membership fees. Fees paid by artist-members vary, generally ranging from $100 and up. In some cooperatives, members pay a one-time initiation fee plus a flat fee, depending upon the shows in which their work is exhibited. Others charge dues at various agreed-upon time intervals.

C o-op galleries resemble retail galleries except that business aspects are shared among the member artisans. Like retail galleries, co-ops appear in all shapes and sizes. To gain the privilege of displaying artistic work in a co-op gallery, contributions must be made by all participants in order to maintain the gallery. The existence of cooperative galleries depends on artists' active participation. Artisans operate a cooperative gallery, sharing in expenses in return for a guaranteed number of one-person shows as well as group exhibitions, within a specified time period. These gallery artists execute all the managerial decisions, including selection of new artists for membership. Membership in a cooperative is usually initiated by submission of a completed application, which should include slides or photographs of the artisan's finest artwork. The portfolio is then juried by a committee made up of cooperative members. High-quality workmanship is the primary consideration when selecting new members.

Members in a cooperative enjoy many advantages. Artists interact with each other within a well-organized support system gaining useful experience while exhibiting their work. Additional benefits of cooperatives:

- The more experienced craftspeople in the co-op assist the less-experienced members by sharing or trading their advice and knowledge. This supportive arrangement is valuable to beginners who want to learn how to sell their work.

- The co-op setting offers a valuable opportunity to market arts and crafts at a lower cost.

- The cost of materials is divided. When artists have to buy all their own chemicals, glazes, clay, and other essential materials, costs can quickly become prohibitive. Pooling expenses among co-op members can dramatically reduce costs.

- An artist does not have to shoulder all responsibility alone. A person's morale can benefit immeasurably by joining a community of like-minded individuals with every member energetically supporting the group projects.

- Other pluses include shared operating expenses and shared gallery-sitting responsibilities, as well as the sharing of techniques.

Co-ops showcase talent by furnishing a built-in working support system. There may be lots of work and thought required in operating a co-op gallery, but there is satisfaction in being your own boss, making decisions, experiencing the benefit of mutual support, and having direct control over the future.

SPECIAL FEATURES: The participatory structure of the cooperative system offers artists a rare opportunity to control, organize, and choreograph their own exhibitions. The nature of cooperatives requires that they must be directly

David Beathard
"Strange Tree" (Ceramic Vase)
Photo: David Beathard

involved in formulating goals, priorities, and future directions of their member-owned gallery.

QUESTIONS TO ASK:

Can you send me information about your co-op?
When was your co-op established?
What types of artwork are featured?
How often does a member have to pay dues?
How many members are in the co-op?

NEWSLETTER:

The Artisan's Commonwealth is a new quarterly newsletter for and about artisan cooperatives. For more information, contact:
Stephen Clerico
P.O. Box 192
Free Union, Virginia 22940
(804) 978-4109

BOOKS AND BOOKLETS:

How to Start and Run a Successful Handcraft Co-op in Your Own Community
Catherine Gilleland
134 Boston Road
Chelmsford, Massachusetts 01824

Cooperative Approach to Crafts, How to Start a Cooperative, and *The Cooperative Approach to Crafts for Senior Citizens*, are booklets available from:
The U.S. Department of Agriculture
Agriculture Cooperative Service
Washington, D.C. 20250

Kathleen A. Cancilla
Oragami Fan Style Earrings
(Made with Handmade Washi
Paper)
See related information in
Chapter 32
Photo: Dynamic Focus Photography
©1992

Cooperatives:
A Historical Perspective

The cooperative gallery is becoming more and more popular today, although selling arts and crafts by this method is not a recent development. Co-ops came into prominence in New York City after World War II, rendering an imaginative alternative to the dealer-gallery system. During that period of time, relatives and friends frequently assisted artist-members, who performed the installation work and staffed co-op galleries on a rotating basis.

Co-ops may be started by an existing artists' organization or by a group of artists who want to arrange exhibition space for their works of art. They come in all sizes, but all entertain the same goal—sale of their work. Advantages of belonging to a particular co-op are guaranteed gallery space, group shows, and even additional prestige.

Over time each co-op evolves differently. One of the oldest member-owned cooperatives in America is the Blue Ridge Hearthside Crafts Association, formed in 1968. They began as a small group of craftsmen wholesaling their work around the North Carolina countryside. Within three years, this ambitious group began organizing craft fairs. By the early 1970s a retail store was established, and in 1989 a second retail store was opened.

Located in another rural area of North Carolina, Watermark Association of Artisans, Inc. was established. Its main goal was to better its 430 members' standard of living in Elizabeth City. This cooperative now sells to over five hundred stores nationwide, including J.C. Penney, Neiman Marcus, and Hallmark, and more than fifteen different catalog companies. Their sales total upwards of $250,000 a year; over $130,000 of that amount comes from the co-op's sixteen-page, full-color catalog featuring baskets, dolls, wreaths, quilted items, and wood products.

On the other side of the country, the Northwest Gallery of Fine Woodworking opened ten years ago in the heart of Seattle, Washington, in the historic Pioneer Square district. It has opened a second gallery, a few miles east of Seattle in the rapidly growing suburban community of Issaquah. Craft items on display range in size from miniature wooden goblets to large pieces of furniture running the gamut in price from $5 to $5,000. This more traditional form of co-op was modeled after a co-op halibut fishery in Alaska. There are thirty-four owner-members. Each has one share in the business and one vote on the board.

Many times, cooperatives operate from interesting local landmarks, thus successfully capitalizing on the tourist trade. Homespun Gatherings began in June 1987, when a group of local craftspeople combined talents to conduct a home and crafts tour in the small city of Newburyport, about thirty miles north of Boston. Twenty craftspeople tapped into the lively tourist trade by setting up shop in five attractive homes for one day only, displaying wares both indoors and in the gardens. At least a thousand visitors toured the homes, watched the craftspeople at work, and purchased items immediately. When members of Homespun Gatherings discovered that a large retail space was going to be vacated in The Tannery (a newly renovated building turned into retail space), thirteen members negotiated a long-term lease.

The Torpedo Factory in Old Town Alexandria, Virginia's Historic District near Washington, D.C., accommodates five cooperative galleries. This converted factory located on the waterfront next to the Potomac River was built in 1918 for manufacture of torpedo shell cases and functioned nonstop until World War II was over. More than 750,000 visitors annually watch more than 150 artists at work.

Another interesting site is a converted shoe factory in Ephrata, a rural town of twelve thousand in the heart of central Pennsylvania's Dutch country. The

Margaret-Ann Clemente
"Rattles for the Imagination"
See related information in
Chapter 32
Photo: Dynamic Focus Photography
©1993

Artworks at Doneckers is comprised of seventeen thousand square feet, including studio, gallery, classroom, cafe, and exhibition space.

Co-ops often open their doors not only to visitors but to other artists as well. The only cooperative gallery in Dallas, Texas, has been in existence for thirteen years, establishing 500X Gallery as one of the oldest surviving art spaces in the city. In 1992, 500X Gallery began holding an annual competition open to any artist living in the United States.

....

For more information on locating co-op opportunities:

HOW TO CONTACT:

500X Gallery
> 500 Exposition Avenue
> Dallas, Texas 75226
> (214) 828-1111

Craftspeople or artists interested in opportunities with the Artworks can contact:

Artworks at Doneckers
> Marketing Director
> 100 State Street
> Ephrata, Pennsylvania 17522

For a list of informational pamphlets/resources published by Watermark, send a self-addressed, stamped envelope to:

Watermark Association of Artisans
> Number 150
> U.S. Highway 158 East
> Camden, North Carolina 27921
> (919) 338-0853

The Art League is located in the Torpedo Factory, Art Center in Old Town Alexandria. The work of emerging and established artists from the Washington, D.C., area is featured. Established in 1967, The Art League has a membership of nine hundred artists whose exhibited works range from $50 to $5,000. They feature oils, acrylics, watercolors, pastels, pen-and-ink, pencil, mixed media, egg tempera, sculpture, ceramic, fiber, photography, collage, woodcuts, wood engravings, linocuts, engravings, mezzotints, etchings, and serigraphs. For a membership application, contact:

The Art League
105 North Union Street
Alexandria, Virginia 22314
(703) 683-1780

Potomac Craftsmen Gallery is a cooperative association of fiber artists located in the Torpedo Factory Art Center. The co-op has seventy members from the metropolitan area. A wide variety of techniques is represented—handweaving, spinning, dyeing, batik, quilting, felting, papermaking, knitting, and crochet. These craftspeople range from the locally to the nationally known. For information, contact:

Potomac Craftsmen Fiber Gallery
Studio 18
105 North Union Street
Alexandria, Virginia 22314
(703) 548-0935

A colonial building in historical Georgetown is the setting for Spectrum Gallery, a twenty-five-year-old cooperative gallery which features Washington-area artists. Their prices range from $18 to $3,000. They accept oils, acrylics, pastels, watercolors, pen-and-ink, pencil, mixed media, sculpture, ceramic, fiber, photography, collage, woodcuts, etchings, lithographs, and serigraphs. Contact by letter with resumé, slides, and photographs, or call for an appointment:

Spectrum Gallery
1132 29th Street, N.W.
Washington, D.C. 20007
(202) 333-0954

CHAPTER 48

Association Shows and Conventions

PRODUCTS BUYERS WANT: arts and crafts

COSTS TO CONSIDER: booth rental, from $50 on up

More Than Anywhere Else in the World

Americans are joiners. Almost all of us belong to different groups; such as trade associations, professional societies, clubs, veterans groups, and various community organizations. The United States hosts thousands of trade fairs, exhibitions, conferences, and conventions. In fact, there are more meetings held here than in all the other nations combined! There are associations for bridal consultants, professional genealogists, dude ranchers, insurance agents, and art dealers. All of these organizations hold annual meetings at large hotels, convention halls, and other type facilities. Many groups are listed in the *Directory of Conventions* available at larger libraries.

Annual assemblies include a broad agenda of activities, including seminars, side meetings, hospitality suites, and—most important to artists and craftspeople—an exhibit hall where companies display their wares, hold demonstrations, and meet potential customers and clients. Space can be rented where a booth can be set up.

Jewelry artisan Lynne Rutherford has rented a booth at the Texas Music Educators Conference held in Dallas every February for the past three years.

Rutherford begins gearing up for the annual three-day conference immediately after the Christmas selling season ends. Her handcrafted brooches, earrings, and necklaces, all featuring musical motifs guaranteed to enchant conference attendees, range in price from $8 to $40. Rutherford also makes an effort to make valuable contacts so she can get several useful sales leads and referrals from each event. At last year's convention she met a Mary Kay consultant. They decided to collaborate, and now Rutherford alternates giving parties with several Mary Kay consultants, which has proved to be a beneficial sales strategy for everyone involved.

Edie Craig, who teaches special education, and Lynda Ault, a teacher for gifted and talented students, know that it helps their sales of handmade aprons when they attend conventions. They make "educational" aprons specifically designed to carry teaching tools for teachers and librarians. When orders started rolling in for their specially designed $125 aprons on their first day at the Texas School Librarians Association Convention held in Houston, they knew that they were making an item that fulfilled many teachers needs. They produce five differently styled aprons with thematic motifs—Library (the twelve pockets match the Dewey Decimal System), Fantasy (with carousel horses), Western (constructed of look-alike cow material), Explorers (with a ship), and Medieval (includes a sword and magic wand that glows in the dark). Ault says, "The aprons really meet a need for students who are not simply auditory learners. They have to be able to feel things." Ault and Craig want to make learning for children in grades three through eight exciting.

SPECIAL FEATURE: It is difficult to imagine a business, industry, profession, craft, hobby, or other particular interest group that does not have some representative regional or national organization that people could join. In fact, more than two thousand associations maintain headquarters in the Washington, D.C. metropolitan area alone.

Lynne Rutherford
"Call Broadway 5000" (Pin)
Photo: Lynne Rutherford

HOW TO CONTACT: Chambers of Commerce can provide excellent information on any locality. Sometimes their activities have been delegated to other city offices such as visitors' bureaus, convention bureaus, or tourist bureaus. To locate Chamber of Commerce addresses and telephone numbers, contact:

The Chamber of Commerce of the United States

1615 H Street, N.W.
Washington, D.C. 20062
(202) 659-6000

An easy way to locate all types of associations is by consulting *The Encyclopedia of Associations*, which is updated every two years. Each entry lists information such as the size of membership, the headquarter's address, telephone number, and any publications circulated by the organization. *The Encyclopedia of Associations* is separated into volumes:

Volume 1-National Organizations of the United States
Volume 2-Geographic—Executive Index
Volume 3-New Associations and Projects
Volume 4-International Organizations

The encyclopedia is available at most libraries or through:

Gale Research, Inc.

835 Penobscot Building
Detroit, Michigan 48226
(313) 961-2242

Organizing Artists: A Directory of the National Association of Artists' Organizations includes a listing of more than three hundred artists' organizations nationwide. It is available through:

The American Council for the Arts

Department 43
One East 53rd Street
New York, New York 10022
(800) 321-4510, extension 241

The World Almanac has been published annually for a century. Trade association's names, addresses, and number of members are listed. This almanac is available in paperback through bookstores and newsstands, or by contacting:

Gale Research, Inc.
835 Penobscot Building
Detroit, Michigan 48226
(313) 961-2242

National Trade and Professional Associations of the United States and Canada and Labor Unions, published annually, can be found in libraries, hotels, and local Chambers of Commerce. This book is oriented toward the convention business. It not only contains an extensive listing of future meetings and convention schedules, but also has a compilation of key facts about America's seven thousand trade associations, labor unions, and professional societies. Each organization is listed along with its address, phone number, fax number, and executive officer. For information on ordering, contact:

Columbia Books, Inc.
1212 New York Avenue, N.W.
Suite 330
Washington, D.C. 20005
(202) 898-0662

The American Society of Association Executives (an association of associations) can help artisans locate an association that deals with all their possible areas of interest. It is probably better to contact the ones with the most members first. They offer the *Who's Who in Association Management Membership Directory*, which is published annually. For more information, contact:

American Society of Association Executives
1575 Eye Street, N.W.
Washington, D.C. 20005
(202) 626-2723

State and Regional Associations of the United States, 1992, contains information about several thousand of the most significant trade, professional, and labor groups in all fifty states. For information on ordering, contact:

Columbia Books, Inc.
1212 New York Avenue, N.W.
Suite 330
Washington, D.C. 20005
(202) 898-0662

For associations outside the United States:

Directory of Associations in Canada
Micro Media, Ltd.
158 Pearl Street
Toronto, Ontario M5H 113, Canada
(416) 593-5211

Directory of British Associations
CBD Research Ltd.
15 Wickham Road
Beckenham, Kent BR3 2JS
England

Trade Associations and Professional Bodies of the United Kingdom
Pergamon Press, Inc.
Maxwell House
Fairview Park
Elmsford, New York 10523
(914) 592-7700

World Guide to Trade Associations
Saur Verlag KG, Postfach 711009
8000 Munich
Germany
49-89-798901 (telephone number)

Edie Craig and Lynda Ault
Explorer Apron

Yearbook of International Organizations
  Gale Research Company
  835 Penobscot Building
  Detroit, Michigan 48226
  (313) 961-2242

Directory of British Associations and Associations in Ireland
  Gale Research, Inc.
  835 Penobscot Building
  Detroit, Michigan 48226
  (313) 961-2242

Directory of European Associations: Part One: Industrial Trade and Professional Associations
  Gale Research, Inc.
  835 Penobscot Building
  Detroit, Michigan 48226
  (313) 961-2242

Directory of European Associations: Part Two: National Learned, Scientific and Technical Societies
  Gale Research, Inc.
  835 Penobscot Building
  Detroit, Michigan 48226
  (313) 961-2242
  Note: The books listed above can be found in many libraries' reference book sections.

QUESTIONS TO ASK: Do you rent booth space at your conventions?
Is there a waiting list for booth space?
Can you send a schedule of upcoming conferences or conventions?
What products would interest your members?

CHAPTER 49

Selling with Brochures

PRODUCTS BUYERS WANT: arts and crafts

COSTS TO CONSIDER: photography and printing: $100 and up

One of the best ways to convey messages to potential buyers about products is through well-designed brochures that accurately present the artisan's message. However, it can be agonizing to make all the decisions necessary to develop a fine presentation piece that realistically portrays items in the most favorable light possible.

The design of the brochure is limited only by imagination. It can take many forms—from a single sheet to a folder, from a stiff card to a slick promotional piece comprised of several pages. However, because this literature can meet so many sales needs, carefully think through the brochure's intended uses before spending money.

Some brochures take the place of resumés by including education, professional affiliations, collections, and awards. Others communicate only the variety of work done by artisans. Some promotional brochures are totally informational, solely devoted to an artist's background and experience.

Some artisans, like Frances West in Flower Mound, Texas, make their own brochures. She says, "Turning an enjoyable hobby-pastime into a business has been an ongoing learning experience and is hard work. But there came a time when I had to sell my pieces (get rid of them, actually) to support my clay habit." Frances makes fifty brochures at a time that consist of four pages—three pages feature color pictures of her Dalzenstuff, with seasonal favorites such as "Bubba Claus," and a one-page order form. She readily admits that making her own brochures is not a "quick operation, but it is a good and a relatively inexpensive way to introduce one's product(s)."

A brochure can be a pamphlet, booklet, or multifold printed piece. Examples of an artist's work can be presented along with personal background information and career history. The contents may apply to only one market area or can provide a descriptive overview of artistic skills. Consider the following factors when preparing a brochure:

Alyssa Levitan
Hair Ornaments (Handmade
Papers Sculpted Around
Stoneware/Porcelain with
Stones and Beadwork)
See related information in
Chapter 32
Photo: Dynamic Focus Photography
©1992

- ◼ *Collect brochures that are appealing.* Try to discern what makes them appealing. Write down their winning characteristics.

- ◼ *Print pricing information on a separate sheet that will be included later.* If prices have to be changed, the expense of having a new brochure printed can be avoided. So do not have the price of items printed inside brochures.

- ◼ *Many experts suggest that brochures should contain one or more illustrations, preferably in color, that most accurately depict the artist's work.*

- ◼ *Get quotes from notable admirers of artistic work.* Try to obtain the permission of buyers and collectors so their names may be listed as satisfied purchasers. Encourage buyers to give testimonials. Their "glowing endorsements" can be included at a later time in a tasteful manner.

- ◼ *Decide whether or not a business card should be included as part of the brochure.*

- ◼ *Be sure that the brochure prominently displays the correct name, address, and telephone number of the artisan.*

- ◼ *Remember that the brochure portrays a certain image of the artist to the potential buyer.* Make that image complimentary.

- ◼ *Think about creating a brochure that provides helpful information and targets the intended market.* Appeal to the needs of the buyer.

SPECIAL FEATURES: Brochures can be used in many practical ways: at galleries, for museum curators, for interior designers or decorators, for architects, for prospective collectors, for the press, and for publicity.

....

Print shops carry a variety of brochures along with business cards, stationery, and other promotional items. Consult the *Yellow Pages* under "Printers" for nearby shops. Most printers will provide free consultations.

HOW TO CONTACT:

....

Direct Press provides full-color catalogs and catalog tear sheets for more information:

MAIL-ORDER PRINTERS:

Direct Press
9 Dorman Avenue
San Francisco, California 94124
(800) 347-3285 or (415) 641-7600

Direct Press
Century Business Park
2030 Century Center, Suite A
Irving, Texas 75062
(800) 271-7008 or (214) 721-1110, or Fax (516) 271-7008

Dynamic Focus Photography offers studio and location photography in black-and-white and color prints and slides. The studio can assist in the development of promotional materials such as brochures, catalog sheets, postcards, and business cards. Display prints and transparencies for booth exhibits are also available. Contact:

Dynamic Focus Photography
1179 Tasman Drive
Sunnyvale, California 94089
(800) 299-2515

For four-color printing services on photo business cards, postcards, brochures, posters, greeting cards, and reply cards (offers free samples and newsletter) contact:

Lucas Photographics
751 Santa Fe Drive
Denver, Colorado 80204
(303) 595-8301, or Fax (303) 595-4276

For color brochures, booklets, and flyers:

Econocolor
7405 Industrial Road
Florence, Kentucky 41042
(800) 877-7405 or (606) 525-7405

For information about catalogs, catalog sheets, brochures, posters, postcards, statement stuffers, presentation folders, and business reply cards, contact:

Catalog King
1 Entin Road
Clifton, New Jersey 07014
(800) 223-5751, (201) 472-1221, or (212) 979-7100
Fax: (212) 353-9628 or (201) 472-5270

Treaty Oak Press has furnished fine color printing of exhibition catalogs, invitations, art prints, preview sheets, and posters for twenty-eight years. Type and layout can be provided for "a small additional cost." To get printing questions answered feel free to contact the in-house Fine Art Printing consultant at:

Treaty Oak Press
851 Dairy Ashford
Houston, Texas 77079-5301
(800) 327-2162, or in Houston call (713) 497-4661

Ida R. Cutler of The Clay House
"Two Fish Vase" (High-fired
Porcelain with Two Hand
Carved Bone Fish Fetishes
Attached by Leather Thong)
See related information in
Chapter 32
Photo: Dynamic Focus Photography
©1992

Whether you want one thousand or one million, a brochure or a catalog, black and white or full color, Thurston Moore Country, Ltd. offers "complete creative design and quality printing at economical prices." For information about full-color lithography on photo-business cards, postcards, brochures, card posters, and bookmarks, or free samples, write:

Thurston Moore Country, Ltd.
   204 Slayton Drive
   Madison, Tennessee 37115
   (615) 868-7448

QUESTIONS TO ASK:

What is the price range if purchased in large quantities?
What kind of discounts are offered?
How long does it take to get the brochures printed?
What other printing services are offered?
Can you send a brochure or catalog?

BOOKS:

The Complete Guide to Creating Successful Brochures
   Karen Gedney and Patrick Fultz
   Caddylak Systems, Inc.
   Brentwood, New York

The Fine Artist's Guide To Showing and Selling Your Work
   Sally Prince Davis
   North Light Books
   Cincinnati, Ohio

Kathleen B. Shelton
Magnets (Hydrostone Painted
with Acrylic)
See related information in
Chapter 32
Photo: Dynamic Focus Photography
©1993

CHAPTER 50

Craft Malls

Cashing in on the Craft Mall Concept

PRODUCTS BUYERS WANT: arts and crafts

COSTS TO CONSIDER: Rental fees, commissions, and shipping. At least $25 or more.

Rufus Coomer started it all when he began selling crafters' work in 1988 from a converted saw shed at his lumber yard located in Azle, Texas. "The concept has caught on so well," according to Judy Strehe, Coomers marketing manager, "that there are nine stores in the Dallas-Fort Worth area." They estimate that $50 million worth of American crafts will be sold through their craft malls this year. A piece of this enormous market is offered to crafters who can rent space at Coomers for as little as $25 a month. The craft mall concept has evolved into big business.

It is estimated that there are over one thousand craft mall operations located in America. Each is as individual as the owner who rents space. Some are spacious, such as Coomers stores which can be fifteen thousand square feet and are located in Texas, Arizona, Missouri, Georgia, Ohio, Colorado, and Illinois. Others flourish near tourist attractions such as the Weeping Willow Arts and Crafts Mall located in Metropolis, Illinois—Superman's hometown. Some, like Crafters Showcase, off Route 17 South in Paramus, New Jersey, thrive by being situated off major highways.

Although the crafters who sell their work through craft mall stores often live nearby, this is not normally a requirement in order to rent space. Once craft work has been accepted, the mall management will arrange and keep up displays for out-of-town participants.

Craft malls generally want high-quality American-made products. Judy Strehe of Coomers says, "We are finding that the public, especially during the holidays, are shopping our stores because they are looking for something that's as unique as the people that they buy for." To ensure maintenance of a constant caliber of good craftsmanship, management asks all applicants to send pictures or samples of their work when they return the mall's application either personally or by mail. Then the managers decide if the store has a need for the items being offered. They also determine whether or not the crafter's work "fits in" with the other displays.

Most shops regulate the number of craft categories. For example, they may only allow a certain number of woodworkers. After that number has been reached, applicants will be placed on a waiting list for future vacancies.

Mark Beck, who is a professional candlemaker as well as owner of the Craft Center in Bennington, Vermont, advises crafters who are sizing up places to do their own interviewing. "It's very important for them to take an interest in where their things are going," Beck says.

Be sure to ask questions about the craft mall operations before making a commitment. Some common areas of concern are:

- *How many crafters rent mall space?* Two hundred crafters are accommodated in the Crafters Showcase in Paramus, New Jersey. The response to their store has been so tremendous that they are planning to open another soon.

- *How much will it cost to sell my work through the craft mall?* At Coomers, the smallest mall space in Azle, Texas, rents for $25. However, the same space in Rolling Meadows, an affluent suburb of Chicago, rents for $70 because of variance in real estate prices. So Coomers' rental rates depend on the area of country where the mall is located.

■ *When and how are crafters paid?* Judy Strehe of Coomers says, "We pay our crafters religiously every other week without fail, because without them we would not be in business."

■ *What will the "display environment" for your crafts be like?* Mark Beck, the owner-operator of the Craft Center in Bennington, Vermont, says, "This building is exemplary of what you would want a place to look like. It's all rough-cut pine; it's got high ceilings; it's got wide, wide aisles; the displays are low so they don't create all the barriers; it's got beautiful new-age music and country music playing on a very good sound system; it's got state-of-the-art daylight spectrum lighting."

■ *What are the shop's hours? Are they open year-round?* "We are open seven days a week," says Robin Hamlin, manager of the Made by Hand Craft Mall store located in San Antonio.

■ *How is the craft mall space arranged?* Strehe says Coomers craft malls are set up with individual booths. Each crafter usually rents a booth area that best accommodates his or her product's size.

■ *How many crafters are displaying work similar to mine?* Most craft malls select work that will make a good product mix for their stores. Coomers has not experienced any problems in choosing crafter's work in various categories. Strehe says, "It just seems to always work out perfectly."

■ *How long has the store been open? Will there be more stores?* Sometimes if space is not available now, the craft mall will be adding more stores in the future. For example, Coomers expects to add ten stores in various states by the end of 1994.

■ *Does the mall offer any special attributes or activities to attract customers?* In the past, the Craft Center in Bennington, Vermont, has asked various crafters to demonstrate the making of their handiwork to draw visitors.

■ *Are there tourist attractions located in the area?* Weeping Willow Arts and Crafts Mall, located in Metropolis, Illinois, is on the tourists' way to Merv Griffin's Casino Riverboat. This draws lots of traffic, according to

Store Manager Ann Burton. Sometimes the location itself draws tourists. "Made by Hand is off of South Padre Island Drive, which is a major strip area in Corpus Christi," explains Robin Hamlin, manager of the store. Lots of tourists visit, "especially in the summer season."

Mark Beck, located in Vermont, says the fall foliage season draws thousands of people some New Englanders call "leaf peepers" to view the outstanding color of the changing of the leaves. This event brings the Craft Center even better business than the Christmas season.

■ *How much and what kind of advertising is done by mall management?* "We try to do a lot of advertising for the crafters," says Robin Hamlin, manager of the Made by Hand Craft Mall Store in San Antonio. They supply brochures to the tourist information center at the United States-Mexico border. It seems that this strategy is effective. They have had visitors from as far away as Scotland and England, who came to shop at the mall because they had seen their brochures at the border.

COOMERS IN ARIZONA, COLORADO, GEORGIA, ILLINOIS, MISSOURI, OHIO, AND TEXAS

"It used to be that church bazaars were the only place where you could get hand-crafted items," says Judy Strehe, Coomers' marketing manager. "We had one particular lady who started out just that way, in a church group. Then when she walked into the Azle mall, she was selling her angels out of her basket even before she could get to her booth." This crafter started out renting the smallest, least expensive booth. She rents space in all nine Metroplex stores. According to Strehe, "She (the crafter) is making megabucks!"

"Most people who start out in this business do not start out thinking that this will be a full-time business. They start out doing projects for their home or for a family member or for themselves just to have something to do with their hands because it's very therapeutic. Then a friend tells them, 'I really think this would sell well' so their hobby develops into a business." Crafters have found that the more malls in which their work is displayed, the better their income, especially considering the state of the economy over the last decade with so many people losing their jobs.

"Last year we started placing ads in trade magazines, and so we are attracting more professional crafters now that do this for a full-time living," says Strehe. Coomers now services over nine thousand crafters. As of early 1994, there were twenty-seven Coomers in seven states—Arizona, Colorado, Georgia, Illinois, Missouri, Ohio, and Texas.

"We're opening a new store in the St. Louis area next month. All the crafters know that they can call Cheryl. We have a crafter coordinator who takes care of all their placements in all of our malls," says Strehe. Coomers Coordinator Cheryl Sharp is happy to help anyone who has questions. "They can call her and ask about any mall. She has statistics on the demographics, so she can get them placed with one phone call.

"We don't want to just sell our space. We want to sell our space with things that are going to sell, that we know our customers want. It doesn't do the crafters any good to sit there and pay us rent if they're not selling anything. We want them to be successful. And their success is our success."

Coomers

6012 Reef Point Lane, Suite F
Fort Worth, Texas 76135
(817) 237-4588

HOW TO CONTACT:

Joei Skesfington, owner of Crafters Showcase in Paramus, New Jersey, says that she and her husband John started their 3,200-square-foot operation because "there were no other stores like this in our area." Sales have been so good that they will soon be opening up another store in Bergen County.

When crafters call seeking information, Skesfington is happy to send out media kit which contains information explaining how their malls operates. The brochure clarifies everything about the store, from pricing of retail space to the kind of advertising done. Crafters Showcase charges a flat monthly rental fee ranging between $75 and $175, depending on the amount of space required. After looking through the materials, crafters can call the store if they have any additional questions.

CRAFTERS SHOWCASE IN PARAMUS, NEW JERSEY

To make certain a crafter's work complements the work of others already in the mall, the owners ask those interested to submit slides (or pictures), make an appointment to come in, or arrange to ship samples of their work for review by the owners. "Some people do mail in their samples; it just depends. It's up to the crafters themselves. Like today, I received some knitted goods through the mail," Skesfington explains. "Photographs often don't come out very well or show nearly any of the quality of the work."

Skesfington says that approximately 70 percent of the participants in Crafters Showcase are from the immediate area, and 20 percent are a couple of states away going out toward New York and New Hampshire. The remainder are nationwide from states such as North Dakota, Ohio, and Missouri. "We've had a lot of inquiries from California and Florida. They tend to have a lot of crafty areas in them, so they have been hearing about us," Skesfington says.

By utilizing the services of a craft mall, Skesfington points out that sellers are "tapping a whole new market" for their work. She does warn crafters, though, "to beware, not to give any money, until they know that the store is functioning and open. We've heard a few horror stories of people taking the money (from crafters who want to rent space), saying, 'I am opening in a month, I need your deposit first,' and then they've never been heard of again." Crafters who rent space should always expect prompt payment of receipts. A warning of possible problems ahead is if they are not getting their checks paid on a timely basis. Skesfington advises crafters to "do their homework" by checking places out before they rent.

"Speak to another crafter or two who sells work through the store," Skesfington says. "For instance, we offer testimonials and referrals with our media kits." Or crafters are welcome to come in and pick cards up from the displays in Crafters Showcase so they can call to ask questions of interest.

HOW TO CONTACT: **Crafters Showcase**
447 Route 17 South
Paramus, New Jersey 07652
(201) 261-6033

Craft Fair USA opened in September 1992. The 11,000-square-foot operation located in a shopping center houses up to 350 crafters. Jennifer Beck says that they welcome all crafters who make American-made goods. There is a play area for shoppers' children, and plans are in the works for adding a cappuccino bar and a gourmet shop. They will send a packet of information that answers questions about their craft mall.

CRAFT FAIR USA IN MISSION VIEJO, CALIFORNIA

Craft Fair USA

25320 Marguerite Parkway
Mission Viejo, California 92692
(714) 707-5900

HOW TO CONTACT:

This craft store is located in Metropolis, Illinois, which proudly displays a statue in Superman's honor in front of the county courthouse. Nearby, a huge country western theater is being built. Merv Griffin's Casino Riverboat was moved into the town's dock on the Ohio River last year. "Because of the casino boat, we get a lot of traffic," Manager Ann Burton explains. "We're right on the main highway just before you get into town—right off Interstate 24 coming out of Paducah, Kentucky." Tourists are drawn from everywhere to these attractions. There are also tour buses that stop.

Open since July 1993, Weeping Willow displays in its store items from three hundred crafters. They have participants from Kentucky, Missouri, Tennessee, Minnesota, Florida, and, of course, Illinois. They are glad to decorate the space for those who are unable to get to the shop. They ask crafters to bring by a sample so they can see their work or, if they are from out of town, to mail pictures. Rent is charged, as well as a 10-percent commission on items sold.

WEEPING WILLOW ARTS AND CRAFTS MALL IN METROPOLIS, ILLINOIS

HOW TO CONTACT: **Weeping Willow Arts and Crafts Mall**
1530-A East Fifth Street
Metropolis, Illinois 62960
(618) 524-5249

MADE BY HAND CRAFT MALLS IN SAN ANTONIO AND CORPUS CHRISTI, TEXAS

"We're trying to widen our crafter base," says Robin Hamlin, manager of the Made by Hand Craft Mall Store in Wurzbach, Texas. "This is so that people who are interested in doing this kind of thing are aware that here is a craft mall that they can work out of."

There are three stores in San Antonio (Wurzbach, Callaghan, and Nacogdoches) and one that is located three hours away in Corpus Christi. "The Wurzbach store is the oldest craft mall in San Antonio," Hamlin says. It has been in business three years. All of the stores are located in shopping strip centers.

"We want quality handmade items," Hamlin says. "We have a lot of people from out of state who have sent pictures or brochures of their things." Some send elaborately designed brochures and others send Polaroid pictures that were snapped in their backyards. "We work off a lease-contract so it's not consignment," she says. "The crafters lease space, like you would an apartment. They pay a monthly rent fee depending on the size of the booth. Our smallest spaces start at $30 a month and then they go up. The largest space goes for $260 a month."

When crafters from Indiana, Arkansas, Colorado, and Ohio, ship their items to the stores, the staff stocks their booths at no extra charge. Some participants, like crafter Judy Mills, who makes Potpourri Scented Pies, have been so successful that they rent space in all four Made by Hand locations.

Made by Hand Craft Mall
3307 Wurzbach
Wurzbach, Texas 78238
(210) 647-1128

Made by Hand Craft Mall
8135 Callaghan
Callaghan, Texas 78230
(210) 341-3785

Made by Hand Craft Mall
12311 Nacogdoches
Nacogdoches, Texas 78217
(210) 656-5091

Made by Hand Craft Mall
4938 South Staples, Suite C-10
Corpus Christi, Texas 78411
(512) 991-6555

HOW TO CONTACT:

"Camelot Village is an entity that is really a half-day stop. That's what makes it so popular," according to Owner Mark Beck. In addition to the Craft Center, housed in a fifty-year-old dairy barn, there is an eighteen-thousand-square-foot antique center, an atrium restaurant, and a collection of country shops. "We're located just outside of town in what is called Historic Old Bennington." Beck goes on to explain the shop's surroundings. Across the street is the Cerniglia Winery which conducts tours and tastings. Next door to the winery is a little schoolhouse, one of the oldest in the state, which is rented out as a Cheese Shop. Close by is First Church with the grave site of Robert Frost. There is also Bennington Area Center for the Performing Arts which houses an art museum, an art gallery, and a theater. All of these tourist attractions appeal to crafters who want to take advantage of the tourist trade by displaying their work at the

THE CRAFT CENTER AT CAMELOT VILLAGE, IN BENNINGTON, VERMONT

Craft Center. Currently, fifty crafters are waiting for space. Beck says, "We have national representation. (Sixty percent of the space is rented to crafters who are from all over the United States.) The bulk of that is from the Northeast, 40 percent are from Vermont." Beck always welcomes crafters who want to check out his shop personally. Anyone who is interested can call, and he will send an information package along with an application.

Beck, who spent fourteen years in advertising in New York, enjoys helping crafters with merchandising to make their displays look better. He is always working "to garner more sales for the crafters, because that's what we're in business to do." He admits that as a craftsman he is one of "the last of the true American individualists" and says, "We run the business on two principles— common sense and fairness."

HOW TO CONTACT:	**The Craft Center at Camelot Village** 60 West Road (Route 9 West) Bennington, Vermont 05201 (802) 447-0228

OTHER CRAFT MALLS:	**Brookfield Craft Center** 286 Whisconier Road Brookfield, Connecticut 06804 (203) 775-4526 **Bayou Crafters Mall** 2316 Cypress Street West Monroe, Louisiana 71291 (318) 325-6519 **Tramway Artisans** Route 16 P.O. Box 748 West Ossipee, New Hampshire 03890 (603) 539-5700

American Craft Network

23 Route 206 South
P.O. Box 374
Stanhope, New Jersey 07874
(201) 426-0049

Arts and Crafts Gallery

72 Route 28
West Harwich, Massachusetts 02671
(508) 432-7604

The Craft Gallery

7524 Bosque
Suite I
Waco, Texas 76712
(817) 751-0693

Linda's Arts and Crafts Emporium

4808 Fairmont Parkway
Pasadena, Texas 77505
(713) 998-7879

SPECIAL FEATURES: Selling through craft malls can be a great way to reach a large audience without requiring the craftsperson to actually be present to make the sales. Holiday seasons can be especially lucrative.

QUESTIONS TO ASK:

How long has your craft mall been in business?
How many spaces does your craft mall rent out?
What are the sizes and prices?
What are your hours of operation?
Are you open year-round?
Do you restock displays for crafters?
Do you accept credit cards?
Who takes care of any sales tax?

How often are crafters paid?

Can you send me information about your craft mall, along with an application?

Bibliography

Bly, Robert W. *Create the Perfect Sales Piece: A Do-It-Yourself Guide to Producing Brochures, Catalogs, Fliers, and Pamphlets*. New York: John Wiley and Sons, Inc., 1985.

Brabec, Barbara. *Creative Cash: Making Money with Your Crafts, Needlework, Designs, and Know-How*. 4th ed. Huntington Beach, California: Aames-Allen Publishing Company, 1986.

Brabec, Barbara. *Homemade Money: The Definitive Guide to Success in a Home Business*. White Hall, Virginia: Betterway Publications, 1992.

Brabec, Barbara. *A Treasure Trove of Crafts Marketing Secrets*. 2d ed. Naperville, Illinois: Barbara Brabec Productions, 1988.

Buxton, Gail. *Craft Making for Love or Money*. New York: Executive Communications, Inc., 1983.

Caplin, Lee Evan. Ed. *The Business of Art*. Englewood Cliffs, New Jersey: Prentice-Hall, Inc., 1982.

Casewit, Curtis W. *Making a Living in the Fine Arts*. New York: Macmillan Publishing Company, Inc., 1981.

Chamberlain, Betty. *The Artist's Guide to the Art Market*. 4th ed. New York: Watson-Guptill Publications, 1983.

Cochrane, Diane. *This Business of Art*. New York: Watson-Guptill Publication, 1989.

Crawford, Tad. *Legal Guide for the Visual Artist: The Professional's Handbook*. New York: Hawthorn Books, 1977.

Davis, Sally Prince. *The Fine Artist's Guide to Showing and Selling Your Work*. Cincinnati, Ohio: North Light Books, 1989.

Davis, Sally Prince. *The Graphic Artist's Guide to Marketing and Self-Promotion*. Cincinnati, Ohio: North Light Books, 1987.

DuBoff, Leonard D. with Michael Scott, Ed. *The Law (in Plain English) for Craftspeople*. Seattle, Washington: Madrona Publishers,1984.

Franklin-Smith, Constance. *Art Marketing Handbook for the Fine Artist*. Renaissance, California: ArtNetwork, 1992.

Frischer, Patricia and Adams, James. *The Artist in the Marketplace: Making Your Living in the Fine Arts*. New York: M. Evans and Company, Inc., 1980.

Gedney, Karen and Fultz, Patrick. *The Complete Guide to Creating Successful Brochures*. Brentwood, New York: Caddylak Systems, Inc., 1988.

Genfan, Herb and Taetzsch, Lyn. *How to Start Your Own Craft Business*. New York: Watson-Guptill Publications, 1974.

Gerhards, Paul. *How to Sell What You Make*. Harrisburg, Pennsylvania: Stackpole Books, 1990.

Goodman, Calvin J. *Marketing Art: A Handbook for Artists and Art Dealers*. Los Angeles, California: Gee Tee Bee, 1972.

Greenwood, Douglas McCreary. *Art in Embassies: Twenty-Five Years at the U.S. Department of State*. Washington, D.C.: Friends of Art and Preservation in Embassies, 1989.

Grant, Daniel. *On Becoming an Artist*. New York: Allworth Press and American Council for the Arts, 1993.

Hart, Russell. *Photographing Your Artwork: A Step-By-Step Guide to Taking High Quality Slides at an Affordable Price*. Cincinnati, Ohio: F & W Publications, North Light Books, 1987.

Hoover, Deborah A. *Supporting Yourself as an Artist: A Practical Guide*. 2d ed. New York: Oxford University Press, 1989.

Hynes, William G. *Start and Run a Profitable Craft Business*. Canada: ISC Press, 1990.

Katchen, Carole. *Promoting and Selling Your Art*. New York: Watson-Guptill Publications, 1978.

Klayman, Toby Judith with Cobbett Steinberg. *The Artists' Survival Manual: A Complete Guide to Marketing Your Work*. 2d ed. New York: Charles Scribner's Sons, 1987.

Levine, Michael. *Guerilla P.R.* New York: HarperCollins Publishers, Inc., 1993.

Long, Steve and Cindy, *You Can Make Money from Your Arts and Crafts*. Scotts Valley, California: Mark Publishing, 1988.

Michels, Caroll. *How to Survive and Prosper as an Artist*. 3d ed. New York: Henry Holt and Company, An Owl Book, 1992.

Ramacitti, David F. *Do-It-Yourself Publicity*. New York: AMACOM, 1990.

Ratliff, Susan. *How to be a Weekend Entrepreneur: Making Money at Craft Fairs and Trade Shows*. Phoenix, Arizona: Marketing Methods Press, 1991.

Scott, Michael. *The Crafts Business Encyclopedia: The Modern Craftsperson's Guide to Marketing, Management, and Money*. 2d ed. Revised by Leonard D. DuBoff: Orlando, Florida: Harcourt Brace and Company, 1993.

Seitz, James E., Ph.D. *Selling What You Make: Profit From Your Handicrafts*. Blue Ridge Summit, Pennsylvania: TAB Books, 1993.

Smith, Allan H. *How to Sell Your Homemade Creation*. Orangevale, California: Success Publications, 1984.

Todd, Alden. *Finding Facts Fast*. 2d ed. Berkeley, California: Ten Speed Press, 1979.

Truesdell, Bill. *Directory of Unique Museums*. Phoenix, Arizona: Oryx Press, 1985.

Wolf, Jack S. *Export Profits: A Guide for Small Businesses*. Dover, New Hampshire: Upstart Publishing Company, Inc., 1992.

Woods, Mary. *Turn Your Hobbies into Cash*. San Francisco, California: MWS Publications, 1981.

Articles

Allen, Jim. "Retail Outlets for Crafts at Malls—Kiosks, Pushcarts, and Temporary Storefronts." In *The Crafts Report* (October 1988): 18.

Amt, Kathleen, Manchester, Judy, McDonough, Marcia, and Spiller, Ellen. "What Are the Benefits of Cooperatives?" In *The Crafts Report* (July 1992): 3.

Bell, Eddie. "Jewelry Manufacturer Questions Use of Popcorn as Alternative Packing Material." In *The Crafts Report* (September 1991): 15.

Clerico, Stephen A. "Creating Locally, Thinking Globally: Finding a Place for the Co-op Process." In *The Crafts Report* (July 1992): 3.

Conner, Susan. "Artist's Market: Where and How to Sell Your Art." In *The Artist's Magazine* (September 1987): 14-22.

Di Francesco, Alexandra. "Seasonal Boutique Mystique." In *The Front Room News* (January 1989): 7-8.

Emery, John C. "Build Business by Joining Your Local Builders Association." In *The Crafts Report* (March 1990): 27.

Golletz, Morna McEver. "Artworks Fits into Converted Shoe Factory." In *The Crafts Report* (February 1990): 10.

Gustafson, Paula. "Package Design is More Than Just a Container." In *The Crafts Report* (July 1991): 15.

Hersey, Jan. "Contracting with the Corporate World." In *The Crafts Report* (October 1991): 23-25.

Hersey, Jan. "Craftspeople are Working Their Way into the Corporate Art World." In *The Crafts Report* (October 1991): 1, 22-23.

Meltzer, Steve. "A Look at a Woodworkers' Cooperative That Works." In *The Crafts Report* (February 1991): 1, 1,

Oregon Potters Association Newsletter, June 1988.

Osburn, Denise. "Evaluate Your Business Card: Does It Do Its Job?" In *The Crafts Report* (October 1991): 15.

Pieroway, P. Ann. "International Trade: Preparing Quotes and Handling Inquiries." In *The Crafts Report* (March 1990): 13.

Pieroway, P. Ann. "Public Relations Offers Instant Credibility." In *The Crafts Report* (January 1991): 1, 20-22.

Pieroway, P. Ann. "Selling to Overseas Markets Can Be Profitable If You Do Your Homework." In *The Crafts Report* (January 1989): 16.

Pieroway, P. Ann. "Thinking of Exporting? Research the Various Channels of Distribution." In *The Crafts Report* (December 1989): 18.

Radeschi, Loretta. "Think of Your Business Card As A Miniature Billboard." In *The Crafts Report* (October 1991): 15.

The Crafts Report. "Restaurants Can Be a Very Good Market for Potters." (January 1989); 46.

The Crafts Report. "Short Takes." (March 1991); 50.

Thuermer, Karen E. "Europe." In *The Crafts Report* (January 1993): 11-12.

Townsend, Milon. "Packaging Your Craft Products for Shipping Is No Simple Task." In The Crafts Report (November 1991): 1, 11.

Yarrow, Christine. "On-Line Network to Link Arts Groups Across Country." In *The Crafts Report* (February 1992): 9.

Resources

Magazines:

Airbrush Action
400 Madison Avenue
Lakewood, New Jersey 08701
(908) 364-2111

American Artist
P.O. Box 1213
Newark, New Jersey 07101

Art and Artists
280 Broadway
No. 412
New York, New York 10007

Art Book Review Quarterly
1 Stewarts Court
220 Stewarts Road
London SW8 4UD
England
071-720-1503

Art Business News
P.O. Box 3837
Stamford, Connecticut 06905
(203) 356-1745

Art in America
575 Broadway
New York, New York 10012

Art New England
425 Washington Street
Brighton, Massachusetts 02135
(617) 782-3008

Artforum
65 Bleecker Street
New York, New York 10012
(212) 475-4000

Artist's Magazine
1507 Dana Avenue
Cincinnati, Ohio 45207
(513) 531-2222

ARTnews
48 West 38th Street
New York, New York 10018
(212) 398-1690

Better Homes and Gardens
1716 Locust Street
Des Moines, Iowa
(515) 284-3000

Communication Arts
P.O. Box 10300
410 Sherman Avenue
Palo Alto, California 94303
(415) 326-6040

Corporate Art News
48 West 38th Street
9th Floor
New York, New York 10018
(212) 398-1690

Crafts Magazine
PJS Publications, News Plaza
P.O. Box 1790
Peoria, Illinois 61656
(309) 682-6626

Decorative Artist's Workbook
1507 Dana Avenue
Cincinnati, Ohio 45207
(513) 531-2222

Entrepreneur
2392 Morse Avenue
P.O. Box 19787
Irvine, California 92714
(800) 421-2300

Entrepreneurial Woman
2392 Morse Avenue
P.O. Box 19787
Irvine, California 92714
(800) 421-2300

Equine Art
P.O. Box 1315
Middleburg, Virginia 22117

Equine Images
P.O. Box 916
Fort Dodge, Iowa 50501

Family Circle
110 Fifth Avenue
New York, New York 10011
(212) 463-1799

GATFWorld
Graphic Arts Tech Foundation
4615 Forbes Avenue
Pittsburgh, Pennsylvania 15213
(412) 621-6941

Fiberarts
50 College Street
Asheville, North Carolina 28801
(704) 253-0468

Fine Art Collector
333 North Palm Canyon Drive #206
Palm Springs, California 92262

Good Housekeeping
Hearst Corporation
959 Eighth Avenue
New York, New York 10019
(212) 649-2000

Graphic Design: USA
120 East 56th Street
New York, New York 10022

Illustrator
500 South 4th Street
Minneapolis, Minnesota 55415

Independent Living
Equal Opportunity Publications
44 Broadway
Greenlawn, New York 11740
(516) 261-8917

Ladies' Home Journal
100 Park Avenue, 3rd Floor
New York, New York 10017
(212) 953-7070

McCall's Needlework and Crafts
PJS Publications, News Plaza
P.O. Box 1790
Peoria, Illinois 61656

Michaels Arts and Crafts
1227 West Magnolia, Suite 500
Fort Worth, Texas 76104
(800) 875-3346

Museum and Arts Washington
1707 L Street, N.W. #222
Washington, D.C. 20036
(202) 659-5973

Museum News
1225 Eye Street, N.W.
Washington, D.C. 20005
(202) 289-1818

Niche
Suite 300, Mill Centre
3000 Chestnut Avenue
Baltimore, Maryland 21211
(410) 889-2933

Popular Photography
Hachette Magazines
1633 Broadway, 43rd Floor
New York, New York 10019

Profitable Craft Merchandising
News Plaza
P.O. Box 1790
Peoria, Illinois 61656

Redbook
224 West 57th Street
New York, New York 10019
(212) 649-3450

Southwest Art
P.O. Box 460535
Houston, Texas 77056
(713) 850-0990

Stained Glass Quarterly
6 Southwest 2nd Street #7
Lee's Summit, Missouri 64063

Success
Lang Communications
230 Park Avenue
New York, New York 10169
(212) 551-9500

Sunshine Artists
1700 Sunset Drive
Longwood, Florida 32750
(305) 323-5927

Threads
The Taunton Press
63 South Main Street
Newtown, Connecticut 06470
(203) 426-8171

US Art
12 South 6th Street, No. 400
Minneapolis, Minnesota 55402

WestArt
P.O. Box 6868
Auburn, California 95604
(916) 885-0969

Wildlife Art News
P.O. Box 16246
St. Louis Park, Minnesota 55416

Workbench
KC Publishing
700 West 47th Street #310
Kansas City, Missouri 64112
(816) 531-5730

Newsletters:
Front Room News
P.O. Box 1541
Clifton, New Jersey 07015

National Home Business Report
P.O. Box 2137
Naperville, Illinois 60567

Quilter's Newsletter
Leman Publications
6700 West 44th Avenue
Wheatridge, Colorado 80033

Index

Resource Index

Subject Index